8 DECLARATIONS TO SPEAK OVER YOUR LIFE

The Power of Words for Spiritual Transformation

By

Dr. O. Jermaine Bego, Dmin

ACKNOWLEDGEMENTS

I want to take a moment to acknowledge my beloved CenterPoint Baptist Church, where I have been privileged to serve as Senior Pastor. These declarations were birthed out of our church's Sunday morning Worship service, where we would unite in affirming God's promises over our lives. Through the dedication and faith of our congregation, I have witnessed the transformative power of these declarations, and it is from that foundation that this work was formed. Thank you for your continued love, prayers, and support as we journey together in faith and purpose.

8 Declarations to Speak Over Your Life

The Power of Words for Spiritual Transformation

CONTENTS

PREFACE

In the journey of life, there are moments where the noise of the world can cloud our vision, blurring the path that God has laid out for us. It's in these times that we need guidance, a beacon to lead us back to our purpose. This book, I pray, will be that beacon for you. Here, you will find spiritual, financial, and mental wellness intertwined in a tapestry of daily declarations designed to illuminate your path and elevate your life.

My journey has been one of faith, determination, and relentless pursuit of betterment—not just for myself, but for every soul I have had the honor to guide. As a CEO and Pastor, I have been blessed with the opportunity to witness the transformative power of commitment to community, family, and self.

Throughout my career, I have come to understand that success isn't merely about financial abundance or social status. True success is holistic; it integrates our mental, emotional, and spiritual well-being with our material aspirations. This belief has driven me to compile this book, aiming to provide a framework that you can adopt to bring balance and prosperity into every facet of your life.

In this book, you will find daily declarations sourced from Biblical text, each designed to reinforce a positive mindset and foster your spiritual growth. These declarations are more than mere words; they are affirmations rooted in scriptural truths.

The wisdom imparted in these pages is not mine alone; it is derived from the experiences, teachings, and traditions of our Ancestors as well as contemporary scholars of theology and psychology. I have had the privilege of learning from a diverse spectrum of mentors and institutions, including Massanutten Military Academy, the University of the District of Columbia, Calvary Christian College, The Samuel DeWitt Proctor School of Theology at Virginia Union University, and The Morehouse School of Religion at The ITC. Each of these experiences has enriched my understanding and fortified my commitment to serving you better.

Above all, remember this guiding principle: "GOD IS WE ARE THEREFORE I AM." This profound truth speaks to our interconnectedness and the divine spark within each of us. It is my hope that through the daily practices outlined in this book, you will come to realize your full potential, not just in terms of personal success but as an integral part of a greater community and divine plan.

As you embark on this transformative journey, hold fast to your faith, lean into your perseverance, and never underestimate the power of a declaration. May the teachings within these pages illuminate your path and may your life be a testament to the boundless possibilities that await those who walk in faith and purpose.

INTRODUCTION

In this fast-paced world, where time moves swiftly and demands on our lives mount daily, it becomes essential to take a step back and reflect on what truly matters. Our pursuit of spiritual, financial, and mental wellness should be as intentional as it is passionate. This book aims to be your guide along this transformative journey.

The journey begins with understanding the power of daily declarations. The spoken word has always held great power, a truth recognized by many cultures and solidly grounded in the Scriptures. "Death and life are in the power of the tongue, and those who love it will eat its fruits" (Prov. 18:21). What we declare into the atmosphere can shape our reality in profound ways.

Daily declarations are not magical incantations; they are purposeful affirmations that align our mindset and actions with our deepest values and highest aspirations. By grounding these declarations in Scripture, we invite divine wisdom and strength into every aspect of our lives. Each chapter of this book will introduce you to tailored declarations aimed at enhancing specific areas of your life, steering you toward a holistic approach to success.

To truly comprehend the impact of daily declarations, consider the life and teachings of Jesus Christ. Jesus frequently used declarations to emphasize faith, heal the sick, and release spiritual power. In the same way, our spoken words, fortified by faith, can transform our lives. We will explore how harnessing this power can bring about wisdom, emotional resilience, spiritual growth, financial abundance, and generational wealth.

This book is also an invitation to cultivate a mindset of dependency on God. "And my God will supply every need of yours according to his riches in glory in Christ Jesus" (Phil. 4:19). Trusting in divine provision allows us to live beyond the constraints of our earthly limitations and puts us in a position to receive The Lord's boundless generosity. By understanding and utilizing specific declarations, you will learn to trust in the certainty of God's promises.

Furthermore, a unified philosophy is crucial for achieving a truly successful life. It's not enough to achieve financial wealth if it comes at the expense of your health or mental well-being. Likewise, a spiritually rich life should also embrace aspects of practical living and financial stewardship. "Beloved, I wish above all things that thou mayest prosper and be in health, even as thy soul prospereth" (3 John 1:2). This biblical directive reminds us of the importance of integration.

With the sections of this book meticulously designed, you will find that each chapter builds on the previous one, offering a clear roadmap to integrating the three unifying principles into your daily life. The declarations provided are meant to be both contemplative and actionable, enabling you to reflect on deeper truths while supplying the impetus to take decisive steps toward your goals.

Your commitment to this process is paramount. Transformation doesn't happen overnight, but through consistent effort and a heart open to divine guidance, profound change is not just possible—it is inevitable. The Bible reminds us, "And let us not be weary in well doing: for in due season we shall reap, if we faint not" (Gal. 6:9). Perseverance, coupled with faith, will see you through.

Let's delve into a profound biblical example that encapsulates the power of declarations: the story of David and Goliath. David's declaration of faith before facing the giant—"This day will the Lord deliver thee into mine hand; and I will smite thee, and take thine head from thee" (1 Sam. 17:46)—was a monumental statement. It was not arrogance but a confident proclamation rooted in his trust in God. This same kind of faith-filled declaration can turn your giants into mere stepping stones toward your destiny.

Remember that the process is deeply personal yet universally applicable. The principles you're about to uncover can benefit anyone, regardless of where they currently stand. By the end of this book, not only will you have imbued your life with wisdom, wealth, and wellness, but you will also have a toolkit of declarations grounded in the eternal truths of Scripture, ready to lead you toward a fulfilling and successful life.

Take a moment to reflect on your current life. Are you truly living up to your potential? Is your life characterized by purpose, health, and abundance? If any part of you feels like it's falling short, then this journey through daily declarations may be the catalyst for your breakthrough.

Finally, remember the promises found in God's Word. "For I know the thoughts that I think toward you, saith the Lord, thoughts of peace, and not of evil, to give you an expected end" (Jer. 29:11). The Lord's plans for you are filled with hope and a future brimming with promise. As you declare His truths over your life, expect to see transformation that goes beyond the natural realm and touches the very core of your existence.

Understanding Daily Declarations

Understanding daily declarations is about harnessing the power of the spoken word to shape your reality. The Bible tells us, "Death and life are in the power of the tongue" (Prov. 18:21), emphasizing that our words hold immense power. Daily declarations are intentional, positive statements made to affirm one's beliefs and intentions. These declarations are not just empty affirmations—they are potent, faith-filled proclamations grounded in biblical truth.

The essence of daily declarations lies in their consistency and foundation. By regularly declaring positive, scripturally based truths over our lives, we nurture and build our faith. The key is to make these declarations a habitual part of our daily routine, thus reinforcing the mindset and behaviors.

Daily declarations serve as a spiritual anchor, grounding us in the truths of God's word amidst life's tempests. When life's challenges arise, our declarations remind us of God's promises and faithfulness. For every situation, there is a divine promise. For instance, Jeremiah 29:11 promises, "For I know the thoughts that I think toward you, saith the Lord, thoughts of peace, and not of evil, to give you an expected end." By declaring such promises, we align ourselves with God's will and purpose for our lives.

A practical way to implement daily declarations is to first identify the areas of your life where you seek change or growth. In essence, understanding daily declarations involves recognizing their role in a transformative journey. Whether it's overcoming fear, achieving professional success, or nurturing personal relationships, declarations create a mental and spiritual framework that supports positive outcome. The act of speaking these truths enforces a belief system that affects not just the mind but the spiritual dimension as well.

Enacting daily declarations requires discipline and faith. It's easy to recite words, but truly believing them can be challenging when faced with contrary circumstances. The ultimate goal of understanding daily declarations is to cultivate a continuous state of spiritual alignment and positive expectancy. As we declare God's promises daily, we are training our minds to think and speak in accordance with The Lord's will. This practice builds inner strength, resilience, and a forward-thinking mindset.

Our words function as seeds sown into the soil of our daily lives. What we declare today has the power to manifest in our future. This is why it's vital to guard our tongues and speak only what aligns with God's word. Implementing daily declarations doesn't require grand gestures. It can start with a few moments each morning or evening, affirming truths over your life. Over time, these moments accumulate, creating a reservoir of faith and positive expectation. Whether spoken in solitude, shared with a loved one, or written in a journal, the act of declaring these truths daily fortifies our spirit.

Finally, the practice of daily declarations is a journey of continual growth. As we immerse ourselves in God's word and speak The Lord's promises, we begin to see tangible changes in our lives. Our mindset shifts, our faith deepens, and we start to embody the truths we declare. This transformative journey leads us closer to achieving the successful, balanced life we seek.

Understanding daily declarations is about recognizing the power of our words and their alignment with biblical truths. By consistently speaking life, faith, and God's promises over our situations, we pave the way for transformative change and holistic success. The foundation of scriptural declarations roots us in divine truth, guiding us through challenges and victories alike.

What Are Daily Declarations?

Daily declarations are more than mere affirmations; they are powerful statements grounded in faith and scripture, designed to align your thoughts, words, and actions with God's will. These declarations serve as a guide to frame your mindset and set the tone for how you approach each day, transforming your belief system steadily and consistently towards Spiritual, Financial, and Mental Wellness.

Think of daily declarations as spiritual GPS coordinates that help you navigate the complexities of life. Just as the Bible states, "Death and life are in the power of the tongue: and they that love it shall eat the fruit thereof" (Prov. 18:21). When we declare God's promises over our lives, we are speaking life, wisdom, and abundance into existence. These declarations remind us daily of our divine nature and connection to a higher purpose.

At their core, these daily declarations are rooted in Biblical scriptures, ensuring that each utterance is imbued with divine authority and grace. By embedding scripture into our daily affirmations, we harness the power of God's word to transform our thoughts, behaviors, and ultimately our lives. Through daily declarations, we're actively participating in God's plan for us, reinforcing our trust in The Lord's perfect design.

The act of making daily declarations isn't about blind positivity or wishful thinking. Rather, it's a disciplined exercise of faith and intentionality. It's about taking your belief in God's promises and translating that belief into the spoken word, thus activating the power inherent in scripture. When wielded correctly, daily declarations can cut through doubt, fear, and negativity, illuminating the path to a life filled with divine favor and spiritual abundance.

Moreover, these eight daily declarations function as both a shield and a weapon. As a shield, they protect against the harmful whispers of doubt and negativity. As a weapon, they strike down opposing thoughts that seek to derail you from your divine purpose. They cultivate a mindset steeped in faith, promoting a lifestyle of continual growth and adherence to God's will. In fact, Isaiah 54:17 powerfully asserts, "No weapon that is formed against thee shall prosper; and every tongue that shall rise against thee in judgment thou shalt condemn." Through daily declarations, we arm ourselves with divine truths that safeguard our minds and hearts.

Why should these declarations be a part of your daily routine? Simple. Consistency in repeating these declarations rewires the brain and improves mental resilience. Just as physical exercise strengthens muscles, spiritual exercise—like making daily declarations—fortifies the mind and spirit, aligning them more closely with God's purposes. Daily declarations also serve as reminders. They remind us of the promises found within scripture, the principles we aim to live by, and the goals we aspire to achieve. They keep our focus fixed on the divine, ensuring that our actions and decisions reflect our spiritual convictions.

Another critical aspect of these eight daily declarations is their role in spiritual warfare. Through daily declarations, we assert our spiritual authority and claim victory over adversities. By declaring God's promises, we resist the enemy's attempts to sow discord and destruction in our lives.

Furthermore, the practice of making these eight daily declarations nurtures a spirit of gratitude and contentment. When we declare God's blessings, we become more aware of The Lord's mercies and goodness in our lives. It becomes easier to see The Lord's hand at work and to appreciate the numerous ways He blesses us. Daily declarations cultivate a heart of thanksgiving, enhancing our overall well-being.

Another beautiful dimension of daily declarations is their universality. Anyone, irrespective of where they are on their spiritual journey, can benefit from these declarations. Whether you're a new believer seeking to ground yourself in faith or a seasoned disciple looking to deepen your spiritual walk, daily declarations offer a potent tool for growth and transformation. The act of declaring God's word over your life transcends age, experience, and circumstance, making it a timeless practice for all believers.

Lastly, let's not forget the transformative power of community in making daily declarations. When groups of believers come together to declare God's word, the collective faith and unity amplify their effectiveness. Incorporating daily declarations into communal prayers and gatherings can foster a deeper sense of fellowship and shared spiritual growth.

Daily declarations serve as a steadfast anchor amid life's tumultuous seas. They remind you of your divine worth, instill wisdom, nurture emotional and mental wellness, fortify spiritual well-being, and provide a roadmap to financial and generational prosperity. As you delve deeper into this book, you'll encounter specific declarations tailored to various aspects of life, all designed to help you achieve Spiritual, Financial, and Mental Wellness.

CHAPTER 1:
UNDERSTANDING YOUR WORTH

Before we embark on this journey, it is crucial to take a step back and recognize our worth. Understanding your worth is not about vanity, but about seeing yourself through the eyes of God. The world may try to diminish you, but remember, you are a child of the Most High.

Pause for a moment and reflect on that truth: you are not here by accident. You are a deliberate creation, fashioned intricately by the Creator. Recognizing your worth starts with embracing this divine truth. It's a foundation upon which you can build a life filled with determination and purpose.

God doesn't make mistakes. Every cell, every trait, every talent you possess is part of The Lord's grand design. People often get caught up in comparing themselves to others, leading to feelings of inadequacy. But the Bible reminds us that each person has their own unique gift from God (1 Corinthians 7:7). You have your purpose, and no one else can fulfill it but you.

When you acknowledge this divine truth—that you were intentionally made and are known intimately by God—you lay the foundation for a life anchored in something eternal and unchanging. This acknowledgment becomes a cornerstone for living with determination and purpose, free from the need for external validation or societal standards.

Understanding that you are intentionally created gives you the motivation to face life's challenges with resolve. It equips you to push forward, knowing that you are here for a reason. This belief helps you persist in the face of obstacles, understanding that your path has a divine purpose. When you know that your life has meaning beyond momentary circumstances, you develop resilience, determination, and an unwavering drive to fulfill your purpose.

Recognizing your worth as a deliberate creation of God also gives clarity to your purpose. You are here to fulfill a unique role that no one else can. Every talent, personality trait, and experience you possess is part of God's grand design, and they are given to you to contribute to your mission in this world. When you accept that your life has meaning, it becomes easier to discern the purpose for which you were created and to pursue it with intention.

Understanding your worth calls for a mindset shift. It demands that you look beyond worldly standards and embrace a heavenly perspective. In a world that values superficial beauty, material wealth, and social status, it's easy to lose sight of what really matters. You must learn to see yourself through the lens of God's unconditional love.

Your worth is intrinsic—you do not need to earn it. It is granted by the mere fact of your existence. This realization can drastically change how you view challenges and obstacles. Knowing that you are valued enables you to face difficulties with a renewed spirit and determination.

Understanding your worth is the first key. Embrace it, live it, and let it propel you towards your divine destiny.

The Value of Determination

Determination is an essential element in understanding your worth. It's the fuel that drives us to overcome obstacles, persevere in the face of adversity, and reach our goals. Being determined means committing to a course of action and seeing it through, no matter how difficult the journey may become. It's this unwavering resolve that shapes our character and solidifies our belief in our own worth.

Determination is not just about pushing through; it's about pushing through because you believe in the value of the goal you're aiming for. Think about Nehemiah, who rebuilt the walls of Jerusalem despite intense opposition: "And I looked, and rose up, and said unto the nobles, and to the rulers, and to the rest of the people, Be not ye afraid of them: remember the Lord, which is great and terrible, and fight for your brethren, your sons, and your daughters, your wives, and your houses" (Neh. 4:14). Nehemiah's determination was anchored in his purpose and faith, illustrating that our determination is often fueled by our belief in the greater good.

The journey to understanding your worth involves recognizing that setbacks and failures are not the end but stepping stones. Sometimes, the path of determination might feel lonely, especially when external validation is scarce. Yet, it's in these moments that we realize our worth is not defined by others' opinions but by our inner conviction and faith. Determination also involves making strategic decisions and sacrifices. Successful people often sacrifice short-term pleasures for long-term gains, fully aware that each step brings them closer to their destiny.

For those who seek to achieve a successful life in wisdom, wealth, and wellness, understanding the value of determination is paramount. It's the thread that weaves through each of these elements, ensuring that our efforts are not in vain. Wisdom requires the determination to continually learn and apply knowledge, wealth needs the perseverance to build and sustain it, and wellness demands the commitment to nurture both body and spirit.

It's easy to forget that small, consistent actions often define our journey more than grand gestures. Whether it's daily affirmations, consistent effort towards a goal, or continuous self-improvement, determination keeps us aligned with our values and aspirations. Being steadfast in our endeavors ensures that the seeds we plant, although they may take time to grow, will eventually bear fruit.

Determination isn't isolated—it influences how we interact with others and can inspire those around us. When people witness your unwavering resolve, it can ignite the same spirit within them. We are called to be the salt and light of the world, therefore, our determination can serve as a beacon, illuminating the path for others and demonstrating that persistence leads to progress.

Determination also leads to a deeper sense of contentment. When you know you've given your all and stayed the course, there's a profound satisfaction that follows, regardless of the outcome. Thus, as you navigate your journey towards understanding your worth, let determination be your anchor.

Set your sights on your goals, trust in the process, and remain steadfast in your endeavors. With this mindset and unwavering determination, you will not only understand your worth but also unlock the abundant life of wisdom, wealth, and wellness that awaits.

Daily Declaration for Powerful Words and Thoughts

Every word you speak is a seed that can produce a harvest—whether for good or ill. When you speak life, you plant seeds of hope, love, and encouragement that can grow into profound blessings. Similarly, speaking words of defeat, anger, or negativity can yield negative outcomes. Today, you choose to speak words of power, backed by divine truth. In doing so, you not only honor God but also create an atmosphere around you that attracts peace, grace, and success.

Before any word leaves your lips, it first forms in your thoughts. The Bible instructs us to renew our minds daily (Romans 12:2), meaning that transformation begins with what we allow into our mental space. When we think on things that are pure and true, our words reflect that purity. Begin by cultivating your inner life—your thoughts and attitudes—so that your words will naturally follow the divine wisdom that's been planted in your heart.

The challenge of controlling the tongue is one of the greatest spiritual disciplines, but also one of the most rewarding. You commit today to watch your speech, knowing that your words can impact not only your life but also the lives of those you encounter. When emotions rise, take a moment to pause, reflect, and ensure that your words are aligned with love and truth.

You are called to be a beacon of light in a world that can often seem dark. Your words have the unique power to uplift someone's spirit, offer comfort in times of distress, and bring hope to situations that seem hopeless. Today, your words will be instruments of healing. You will look for opportunities to speak encouragement into someone's life, recognizing that even the smallest act of kindness through words can create a lasting impact.

I Declare According To Psalm 139:14 That I Am Fearfully And Wonderfully Made

Understanding your worth is foundational to living a successful and fulfilling life, encompassing wisdom, wealth, and wellness. It's a profound acknowledgment that you are created with purpose, intention, and extraordinary design. The Bible verse, Psalm 139:14, says it succinctly: "I will praise thee; for I am fearfully and wonderfully made..." (Ps. 139:14). This is a daily declaration that can transform how you see yourself, ultimately affecting every aspect of your life.

At the core, recognizing that you are "fearfully and wonderfully made" is not merely about self-esteem. It's about understanding the divine craftsmanship in your creation. You are not an accident or an afterthought. The Creator of the universe took time to fashion you with great care and precision. This daily affirmation isn't just a shallow pep talk; it's a deep spiritual truth.

When you declare that you are fearfully and wonderfully made, you speak life into your psyche. By speaking this biblical truth over yourself daily, you're not only reminding yourself of your worth but also aligning your thoughts and actions with God's vision for your life.

It's important to understand that this declaration goes beyond physical appearance; it touches on your entire being. Your thoughts, talents, and the unique attributes that make up your personality are all part of this wondrous design. Embracing this truth encourages you to live authentically and unapologetically. When you know you're crafted intentionally by God, you begin to walk in purpose. You shift from seeking validation in the eyes of others to rooting your confidence in divine affirmation.

This shift in perspective can't be overstated. The world often measures worth by external achievements and superficial standards, but God looks at the heart (1 Samuel 16:7). When you declare that you're fearfully and wonderfully made, you begin to see yourself through God's eyes. This foundational shift impacts your entire outlook on life, creating a positive ripple effect on your decisions, relationships, and aspirations.

Moreover, this declaration fosters resilience. Life is filled with challenges and setbacks, and it's easy to lose sight of your intrinsic worth when faced with difficulties. However, consistently reminding yourself that you are fearfully and wonderfully made bolsters your inner strength. Knowing your worth in God's eyes equips you to face life's adversities with confidence and steadfastness.

Another profound implication of this daily declaration is how it influences your interaction with others. When you embrace your value, you naturally start recognizing the worth in others, too. This can lead to more meaningful and compassionate relationships. By acknowledging your God-given worth, you are better positioned to extend that same respect and love to those around you.

In your career and financial pursuits, understanding your worth is equally transformative. When you know you're fearfully and wonderfully made, you don't settle for less than you deserve. You recognize that you are entitled to opportunities that align with your talents and divine purpose. This is not about arrogance but about honoring the gifts God has uniquely given you. This empowers you to pursue your goals with vigor and faith.

Furthermore, this declaration encourages stewardship of your physical body. Believing you're wonderfully made impels you to take care of your health, understanding that your body is a temple of the Holy Spirit, as mentioned in 1 Corinthians 6:19. Proper nutrition, exercise, and rest become acts of worship and gratitude for the incredible vessel God has given you.

It also nurtures mental and emotional well-being. The mind is a battleground, and self-doubt is a common weapon the enemy uses. By daily declaring you are fearfully and wonderfully made, you guard your mind with truth. This practice not only uplifts your spirit but also cultivates a mindset geared towards positivity and resilience.

Lastly, this daily declaration strengthens your spiritual wellness. It is a form of worship and gratitude to acknowledge God's handiwork in you. The Psalmist exemplifies this grateful heart, "I will give thanks unto thee, O Lord, among the peoples: and I will sing praises unto thee among the nations" (Ps. 57:9). This gratitude loops back into a positive cycle, enriching your spiritual life and drawing you closer to God.

To embrace the declaration that you are fearfully and wonderfully made is to accept God's love and craftsmanship in your life fully. It's more than just daily affirmation; it's a powerful, transformative truth that touches every area of your existence. Speak it, believe it, and let it mold you into the person God intended you to be.

Recognizing that you are fearfully and wonderfully made means understanding that you are designed with intention and purpose. This awareness brings a sense of inherent worth and dignity, stemming from the recognition that you are a unique creation of God, crafted with care and love. This realization is not just a fleeting feeling but a foundational truth that can reshape your self-perception and outlook on life.

In essence, embracing the declaration that you are fearfully and wonderfully made is a holistic approach to wellness. It integrates spiritual, financial, and mental aspects of your life, creating a balanced and fulfilled existence. This truth empowers you to live authentically and purposefully, reflecting the love and craftsmanship of your Creator in all you do.

Wellness Points:

1. Daily Affirmation: Declare according to Psalm 139:14 that you are fearfully and wonderfully made.

2. Self-Reflection: Take time to reflect on your unique talents and gifts, recognizing them as part of your divine worth.

3. Mindfulness Practice: Engage in mindfulness practices that reinforce your intrinsic value and purpose.

4. Positive Environment: Surround yourself with people and environments that affirm your worth and encourage your growth.

5. Gratitude Journaling: Keep a gratitude journal to remind yourself daily of your blessings and accomplishments.

Wellness Questions:

1. How do you remind yourself daily that you are fearfully and wonderfully made according to Psalm 139:14?

   ____

   ____

   ____

2. What steps do you take to ensure that your determination aligns with your divine purpose?

   ____

   ____

   ____

3. How do you handle moments of self-doubt and realign yourself with your intrinsic worth?

   ____

   ____

   ____

4. In what ways can you cultivate a mindset of worthiness and divine purpose in your daily life?

   ____

   ____

   ____

5. How do you incorporate positive affirmations into your routine to reinforce your sense of worth?

   ____

   ____

   ____

Wellness Notes:

CHAPTER 2:
WISDOM FOR EVERYDAY LIVING

Wisdom is more than just knowledge; it is the art of applying life's lessons with grace and discernment. In our bustling lives, the need for wisdom has never been greater. The Bible teaches us that "wisdom is the principal thing; therefore get wisdom: and with all thy getting, get understanding" (Prov. 4:7). This directive establishes a blueprint for everyday living, guiding us through our decisions and interactions with others.

Life brings with it complexities that can often cloud our judgment. Whether it's managing family dynamics, making career choices, or simply balancing our well-being, wisdom acts as our compass. We are called to navigate these waters with prudence. Seeking wisdom is an ongoing journey, one that necessitates reflection and deliberate action.

Sometimes, the simplest actions reveal the depth of our wisdom. Listening more than speaking, exhibiting patience in trying moments, and understanding perspectives different from our own are manifestations of a wise heart. Each day presents an opportunity to practice wisdom, enhancing our daily interactions.

True wisdom is inseparable from humility. Recognizing our limitations and seeking counsel from others is a sign of strength, not weakness. Asking for help isn't an admission of failure but a step towards growing wiser. This humility allows us to learn and evolve consistently.

Wisdom often involves making decisions that might not bring immediate gratification but contribute to long-term well-being. It's choosing integrity over convenience, and quality over quantity. Wisdom for everyday living isn't an abstract concept but a tangible practice. It requires us to be intentional, reflective, and ever-seeking of God's guidance. By integrating Biblical wisdom into our daily routines, the path to a fulfilling life becomes clearer. Let us therefore commit to cultivating wisdom, embodying its principles in all we do, and allowing it to shape us into our best selves.

As you move forward, commit to actively seeking and embodying wisdom in all that you do. Let it influence how you approach challenges, relationships, and opportunities, knowing that it is through wisdom that we can grow into the best version of ourselves—people who reflect God's light and love in the world. When we make wisdom a part of our daily lives, we set the foundation for a life filled with purpose, peace, and divine fulfillment. Therefore, let wisdom be the anchor that steadies you and the guiding principle that shapes you, as you walk the path of becoming all that God has intended you to be.

By embodying wisdom, we become a reflection of God's light in the world. Others will be drawn to the peace and clarity we possess because it is grounded in divine wisdom. Embodying wisdom also allows us to become role models for others, teaching them how to live with integrity, purpose, and discernment.

Cultivating Wisdom

Wisdom is akin to a garden; it demands regular care, attention, and nurturing. At its core, wisdom starts with a reverence for the Divine. Proverbs 9:10 says, "The fear of the Lord is the beginning of wisdom: and the knowledge of the holy is understanding." This kind of fear is not about being scared; it's about profound respect and awe. It's about recognizing that our own understanding is limited and that there's a higher wisdom we can lean on in times of uncertainty.

Another facet of wisdom is discernment—the ability to judge well. Discernment helps us navigate life's choices, from significant life decisions to everyday interactions. It teaches us when to speak and when to listen, when to act and when to be still. In the practical world, wisdom manifests through our actions and decisions. It is seen in how we manage our time, relationships, and resources. A wise person understands the value of time and uses it meaningfully. They nurture relationships with love and respect, and manage resources with an eye for stewardship, knowing that everything they have is ultimately a gift from God.

Wisdom also involves the practice of reflection. Taking time to pause and ponder over our experiences allows us to derive lessons from them. By reflecting on our days and numbering them, we grow in wisdom, appreciating the finite nature of our earthly journey and making each moment count.

Another key practice in cultivating wisdom is seeking wise counsel. No one achieves wisdom in isolation. God places mentors, friends, and spiritual guides in our lives to offer insights and perspectives that we might not see on our own.

Forging a relationship with the Word of God is indispensable in this cultivation. "Thy word is a lamp unto my feet, and a light unto my path" (Psalm 119:105). The Scriptures provide not merely rules or historical accounts but living wisdom that guides every area of life. As you imbibe these eternal truths, you are not just collecting information but transforming your life.

But cultivating wisdom is not without its challenges. The process often involves discomfort as it calls for self-examination and change. Nonetheless, these are growing pains, the kind that lead to maturity and a deeper understanding of life. Trusting in God through the process ensures that we emerge wiser and better. Moreover, wisdom equips us to deal with life's inevitable storms. In Matthew 7:24-25, Jesus speaks of the wise man who built his house upon the rock. When the floods came, the house stood firm because it was founded on a solid foundation. Likewise, wisdom prepares us to weather life's challenges, ensuring that we remain steadfast and unshaken.

Wisdom also fosters resilience. It teaches us that setbacks are not the end but opportunities for growth. Romans 5:3-4 reminds us, "And not only so, but we glory in tribulations also: knowing that tribulation worketh patience; and patience, experience; and experience, hope." Wisdom enables us to harness every experience, good or bad, turning it into a stepping stone on our journey.

In our relationships, wisdom teaches us to love unconditionally, forgive freely, and strive for harmony. It reveals the power of words and the importance of speaking life and positivity into the lives of others. By exercising wisdom in our interactions, we build stronger, more meaningful connections.

To sum up, the journey of cultivating wisdom is ongoing. It's a lifelong pursuit that enriches every aspect of our lives. It calls for a humble heart, a teachable spirit, and a willingness to learn from both the Divine and the everyday experiences that shape us.

May our lives be a testament to the wisdom we gather, reflecting God's light and love in all we do.

Daily Declaration for Wisdom

To fully appreciate wisdom, it's important to understand the distinction between knowledge and wisdom. Knowledge is about gathering facts, data, and information. It is the intellectual understanding of concepts, principles, and truths. For example, a person might have extensive knowledge of science, business, or theology, but without wisdom, they might not know how to apply that knowledge effectively in their own life or to the benefit of others.

Wisdom, on the other hand, is the practical application of knowledge. It is knowing when and how to use the information you have acquired. Wisdom enables you to discern the right path, make sound decisions, and act with integrity and foresight. It helps you see the broader implications of your choices, weigh the consequences, and prioritize actions that align with deeper principles.

While knowledge is important, wisdom transforms knowledge into action that brings about growth, healing, and purpose. Where knowledge can make one appear intelligent, it is wisdom that brings true understanding, compassion, and effective leadership. It allows us to bridge the gap between theory and reality, ensuring that our knowledge leads to outcomes that benefit not only ourselves but also those around us.

I Declare According To Proverbs 4:23 Control Over My Thoughts, Words And Ways

As we delve deeper into understanding wisdom for everyday living, it's crucial to anchor ourselves in one of the most powerful Proverbs, specifically Proverbs 4:23: "Keep thy heart with all diligence; for out of it are the issues of life." This verse emphasizes the profound importance of guarding our hearts, which, in biblical language, often signifies the center of our thoughts and deepest inclinations.

Daily declarations are powerful tools for aligning our minds and actions with divine wisdom. Declaring control over our thoughts, words, and ways according to Proverbs 4:23 isn't just a routine—it is a profound commitment to live intentionally and righteously. Our thoughts are the seeds from which our words and actions grow. To maintain control over our thoughts is to cultivate a garden that produces life-affirming words and actions.

First, let's consider the control of our thoughts. The mind is a battlefield, where decisions that shape our lives are constantly being made. We must vigilantly direct our thoughts toward what is good, noble, and pure. Filtering out negativity and focusing on constructive, uplifting thoughts requires constant effort and divine assistance. By declaring, "I control my thoughts," you acknowledge the God-given ability to choose your mental focus. You invite God's guidance to help you cultivate a mindset that reflects The Lord's wisdom.

Words are the manifestation of our thoughts and have the power to build up or destroy. When we declare control over our words, we take responsibility for their impact. Whether spoken in anger or in love, words can influence not just our lives, but the lives of those around us.

Moreover, controlling our ways—the choices we make and the paths we follow—is vital. This declaration is a commitment to God's leadership, trusting that The Lord's plans and directions far exceed what we could ever orchestrate. Acknowledging The Lord in all our ways means seeking The Lord's wisdom in all that we undertake, ensuring that our actions align with The Lord's divine will.

This trinity of control—thoughts, words, and ways—creates a harmonious balance that illustrates a life steeped in wisdom. It's not just about controlling these aspects of our lives for the sake of control but nurturing them so they align with divine truth and purpose. A person who exercises control over their thoughts, words, and ways, aligns their life more closely with the principles of wisdom outlined in Proverbs. The daily declaration serves as a constant reminder and reinforcement of this alignment.

Understanding this declaration's significance offers a pathway to leading a life ripe with wisdom. The words of Proverbs 4:23 serve as a safeguard, encouraging us to diligently oversee the most intimate areas of our lives. To declare is not merely to state, but to affirm with conviction, giving weight and intentionality to our words and actions. When we declare control over our thoughts, words, and ways, we are essentially setting the tone for a life that reflects God's wisdom.

To integrate this declaration into your daily life, start with meditation and prayer. Reflect on the times when your thoughts, words, and ways either contributed to success or led you away from it. Seek divine guidance and strength in these areas, asking God to illuminate the paths where you need more control and wisdom. In doing so, you open yourself to divine correction and growth.

Consider journaling your experiences and reflections as part of this daily declaration process. Documenting how you exercise control over your thoughts, words, and ways can provide ongoing insight into your spiritual and personal journey. When you notice improvements or challenges, revisit Proverbs 4:23, allowing its wisdom to steer you back on course. Another practical approach is to create a physical or digital reminder of your daily declaration. Place it somewhere visible, such as your bathroom mirror or your computer screen. This constant visualization helps to integrate the declaration into your daily routine, making it a habitual part of your thought process.

Engaging in community or small group discussions about Proverbs 4:23 can also enhance your understanding and application of this daily declaration. Sharing insights and receiving encouragement from others strengthens your commitment and broadens your perspective on how to effectively control your thoughts, words, and ways.

This declaration is a powerful, intentional act of aligning yourself with divine wisdom. By embracing this daily practice, you open your heart to the riches of God's guidance, ensuring that the issues of life that flow from within you are marked by righteousness, peace, and wisdom. This is not a one-time event but a continuous journey of growth and alignment with God's will.

This declaration acknowledges that submitting your mind and speech to God's wisdom is not a passive or accidental experience; it is a deliberate, mindful act of aligning your internal life with divine principles. It's a form of spiritual discipline that, when practiced daily, opens you to the flow of God's guidance. This guidance is not vague or distant; it is practical, bringing clarity and righteousness to the issues of life, which include your decisions, relationships, and reactions.

Furthermore, it's important to recognize that this journey of alignment with God's will is continuous. Just as the heart pumps life throughout the body without ceasing, so must the believer continually seek God's wisdom in every aspect of life. This ongoing process requires intentional reflection and surrender, where each declaration becomes a reaffirmation of your commitment to walk in step with God's wisdom.

By declaring control over your thoughts, words, and actions, you reinforce a life of consistency in honoring God. It reflects a proactive choice to pursue righteousness, peace, and wisdom in all things. Each declaration serves as a spiritual checkpoint, reminding you of the values you seek to embody and the divine wisdom you wish to reflect.

Thus, this daily practice becomes a cornerstone of spiritual growth and maturity. It's about more than self-discipline—it is a divine partnership, allowing God to shape and guide every aspect of your life. Over time, this alignment doesn't just change how you live; it transforms who you are, making your life a testament to God's wisdom and will.

Wellness Points:

1. Daily Declaration: Declare according to Proverbs 4:23 control over your thoughts, words, and ways.

2. Reflection and Meditation: Spend time in reflection and meditation to seek divine wisdom and understanding.

3. Continuous Learning: Commit to lifelong learning and growth, seeking knowledge in all areas of life.

4. Practical Application: Apply wisdom in practical ways, such as managing time, resources, and relationships wisely.

5. Community Engagement: Engage with a community of like-minded individuals who value wisdom and growth.

____
____
____
____
____
____
____
____
____
____
____
____
____

Wellness Questions:

1. How can you actively seek wisdom in your daily decision-making process?

2. What practices do you engage in to cultivate discernment and understanding?

3. How do you balance seeking counsel from others with trusting your inner wisdom?

4. In what ways can you apply biblical wisdom to your professional and personal life?

5. How do you ensure that your pursuit of wisdom aligns with humility and divine guidance?

Wellness Notes:

____
____
____
____
____
____
____
____
____
____
____
____
____
____
____
____
____
____
____
____
____
____
____
____
____
____
____

Wellness Notes:

Chapter 3:
Nurturing Emotional and Mental Wellness

As we delve deeper into the essence of Spiritual Wellbeing, we must pause and reflect on the importance of our emotional and mental wellbeing. Just as a house cannot stand without a solid foundation, our journey cannot be complete without nurturing our inner self. "A merry heart doeth good like a medicine: but a broken spirit drieth the bones" (Prov. 17:22). Emotional and mental health is paramount for a life filled with joy, purpose, and divine wisdom.

Biblical wisdom teaches us that joy and peace are fruits of the Spirit—treasures that should be diligently cultivated and protected. In Galatians, it is written, "But the fruit of the Spirit is love, joy, peace, longsuffering, gentleness, goodness, faith, meekness, temperance: against such there is no law" (Gal. 5:22-23). These are the compass points for a heart and mind aligned with God's will, guiding us through turbulent times.

One of the essential pillars of nurturing emotional wellness is emotional resilience. Resilience isn't simply the ability to bounce back from adversity; it's the fortitude to face life's challenges with a spirit of perseverance and grace. Life, as we all know, is more a winding path than a straight road. Commit to building a steadfast and resilient spirit, standing firm even when storms rage.

How do we foster this resilience? Through intentional practice of mindfulness and gratitude. Take time every day to count your blessings and acknowledge even the smallest victories. Gratitude helps us shift our focus from what we lack to what we have. This simple practice can transform our perspective and fortify our emotional armor against life's trials.

Now, when it comes to mental wellness, clarity of mind and control over our thoughts are key. Guarding our hearts also means guarding our minds from toxic thoughts. It's vital to consistently renew our minds with positive, affirming declarations and God's truth.

Let's not forget the transformative power of prayer and meditation. Taking moments to be still and connect with the divine opens pathways for peace and insight to enter our hearts. Jesus reminds us, "Peace I leave with you, my peace I give unto you: not as the world giveth, give I unto you. Let not your heart be troubled, neither let it be afraid" (John 14:27). These words underscore the tranquility we can achieve through faith.

Practicing self-compassion is also critical to mental wellness. It's easy to fall into the trap of self-criticism, especially when facing setbacks. But, remember to extend grace to yourself, just as God extends The Lord's grace to you. Understand that it's okay to stumble, as long as you rise again with renewed faith and determination.

Lastly, build strong, supportive relationships. Surround yourself with friends and family who uplift and encourage you. "Iron sharpeneth iron; so a man sharpeneth the countenance of his friend" (Prov. 27:17). Healthy relationships can provide a vital support network, helping you navigate life's complexities with a lighter heart.

Nurturing emotional and mental wellness is a lifelong journey. It requires commitment, practice, and a deep reliance on God's promises. Embrace the tools of gratitude, positive declarations, prayer, self-compassion, and strong relationships.

Emotional Resilience

Emotional resilience isn't just about weathering a single storm, but rather developing the capacity to navigate life's unavoidable trials with grace and strength. The Bible frequently reminds us of this critical aspect of human experience. Emotional resilience is the essence of sustaining that spirit within, embodying strength in times of adversity and peace in moments of calm.

Building emotional resilience starts with a strong foundation of self-awareness. Knowing oneself—their strengths, weaknesses, and triggers—is crucial. It allows us to confront challenges head-on without faltering. Another core component of emotional resilience is the ability to maintain perspective. Life's challenges can often seem insurmountable, but seeing them through the lens of faith can provide a more balanced viewpoint.

Another key aspect is to develop a proactive emotional toolkit. This could include practices such as mindfulness, prayer, and physical activities that enhance mental well-being. Engaging in these practices not only fortifies our resilience but also prepares us to face future challenges with renewed vigor. Understand that consistency is the backbone of emotional resilience. Regularly engaging in activities that nurture our emotional well-being ensures that we remain steadfast. This diligence, this unwavering commitment to our emotional health, sets the stage for overcoming life's storms.

Emotional resilience, after all, isn't an inherent trait that a select few are born with. It's a skill, a habit, an attitude that can be developed and strengthened over time. By anchoring ourselves in faith, cultivating gratitude, seeking community, practicing forgiveness, equipping ourselves with emotional tools, maintaining consistency, and keeping faith at the forefront, we can develop the resilience necessary to thrive, regardless of life's challenges.

Daily Declaration for Mental and Emotional Well-being

Making a daily declaration for mental and emotional well-being is a powerful tool for cultivating a positive mindset and emotional resilience. It involves consciously affirming truths that promote peace, strength, and balance in your life. Such declarations serve as reminders of your inherent worth, capabilities, and the power you possess to face the challenges of each day.

When you begin your day with affirmations focused on mental and emotional well-being, you set a tone of intentionality. You acknowledge that your mental health is a priority and that you have the ability to shape your responses to life's events. This daily practice is more than just repeating positive phrases; it's a deliberate choice to center your thoughts and emotions on what is true, empowering, and life-giving.

A declaration for mental well-being might include acknowledging your capacity to manage stress and anxiety. By affirming that you are in control of your thoughts and that you have the power to shift your mindset, you build confidence in your ability to face the day with calm and clarity. These affirmations might look like: "I am at peace with myself. I have the power to remain calm in challenging situations. My mind is clear, and I am capable of navigating any difficulty with grace."

For emotional well-being, a daily declaration focuses on acknowledging the importance of emotional regulation and resilience. You remind yourself that emotions are a natural part of life, and rather than being overwhelmed by them, you have the ability to observe, understand, and process your feelings in a healthy way. You might affirm: "I embrace my emotions with compassion.

These declarations not only affirm your present state but also guide your intentions for the day ahead. They help you anticipate the inevitable challenges life brings and remind you that, regardless of what happens, you are capable of responding with strength, wisdom, and emotional balance.

Another key aspect of these declarations is the grounding in self-compassion. Mental and emotional well-being requires kindness towards oneself, especially during moments of struggle or doubt. Daily declarations can affirm this by reminding you that it's okay to have bad days and that your worth is not diminished by moments of vulnerability. Phrases like "I give myself grace when I stumble. I am worthy of love and compassion, regardless of my circumstances" reinforce the understanding that perfection is not the goal, but progress and self-acceptance are.

A regular practice of making these daily declarations builds a mental and emotional foundation rooted in positivity, self-awareness, and resilience. Over time, these affirmations shape your internal dialogue, creating a mental environment where peace and strength flourish. Instead of reacting impulsively to stress or emotional triggers, you cultivate a sense of mindfulness, allowing you to respond with intentionality and composure.

A daily declaration for mental and emotional well-being is more than a motivational tool—it is an active step toward nurturing a balanced, peaceful, and empowered mind and heart. It reinforces the belief that you are capable of navigating life's complexities with grace, that your emotions are valid and manageable, and that you possess the strength to overcome challenges.

I Declare According To Galatians 5:22-23 Discernment In My Choices

Nurturing one's emotional and mental well-being is a task that requires intentionality and a heart turned towards wisdom. The chaos and clamor of today's world often create a whirlwind that can cloud our judgment, making it difficult to make decisions that align with our true selves and godly principles. In the context of Galatians 5:22-23, which speaks of the fruit of the Spirit—including love, joy, peace, patience, kindness, goodness, faithfulness, gentleness, and self-control—we find a blueprint for discernment in our choices. The declaration, "I declare according to Galatians 5:22-23 discernment in my choices," is a commitment to living a life steeped in these virtues.

Discernment is more than just making the right decisions; it's about making decisions that reflect the nature of God's Spirit within us. When we declare discernment according to the fruit of the Spirit, this affects everything from our relationships and careers to our personal growth and daily interactions. It's a holistic approach that integrates every aspect of our being—emotional, mental, and spiritual.

Consider the virtue of love as listed in Galatians. When we make decisions grounded in love, we transcend selfish motivations and think about the greater good. This could mean choosing to forgive when wronged or deciding to help someone in need. The love described in Galatians 5:22 is a selfless love, and declaring discernment in your choices involves inviting that love to guide your actions.

Next, think about joy. Joy is not simply happiness that comes and goes with circumstances; it's a deep-rooted state of being that persists even during trials. By focusing on discernment in our choices influenced by joy, we choose pathways and responses that reinforce our internal stability and optimism. This joyful outlook can transform how we handle stress and adversity, directing us towards constructive solutions and interactions imbued with positive energy.

Peace is another essential fruit that aids in discernment. A heart at peace is not easily swayed by fear or anxiety. When we declare our discernment in peaceful terms, we pave the way for decisions that are thoughtful and measured, untainted by haste or panic. Such peace ensures that our choices reflect stillness and clarity, fostering environments of cooperation and mutual respect.

Patience is indispensable for discernment. Many poor decisions are made in haste, driven by the urgency of momentary pressures. When we declare discernment with patience, we allow ourselves the grace to wait, to listen, and to seek God's timing rather than rushing ahead with our agenda. Patience helps us to pause and reflect, facilitating decisions that are not only wise but also aligned with divine timing.

Kindness, too, should guide our discernment. When kindness frames our choices, we approach situations and people with a generosity of spirit. This doesn't mean we become doormats, but rather, we act with a heart inclined towards compassion and understanding. Kindness in our decisions often breeds goodwill and improves our overall emotional landscape.

Goodness, another fruit of the Spirit, pertains to moral integrity and righteousness. Decisions underpinned by goodness are those that honor ethical standards and moral truths, reflecting God's character in our everyday lives. This means choosing honesty over deceit, fairness over prejudice, and righteousness over convenience. When we integrate goodness into our choices, we reflect Christ's nature and uphold principles that ensure long-term blessings.

Faithfulness and discernment go hand in hand. A faithful heart remains steadfast, even when the path is challenging. Faithfulness in our choices means commitment to our values, promises, and God's commandments. This determination ensures that our decisions are not swayed by external pressures or fleeting desires. Faithful decisions endure the test of time and are rooted in trust in God's plan.

Gentleness, a fruit often overlooked, plays a pivotal role in discernment. A gentle approach encompasses humility and self-restraint. When we declare discernment guided by gentleness, our decisions are tempered by consideration and respect for others. This kind of discernment avoids harshness and embraces empathy, creating a ripple effect of positive, gentle interactions in our communities.

Lastly, self-control is vital for true discernment. The ability to exercise control over our impulses and desires ensures that our choices are thoughtful and intentional rather than reactionary. When Paul describes the fruit of the Spirit, he concludes with self-control as it ties all other virtues together. It's the discipline that allows us to act in alignment with all the other fruits. "He that hath no rule over his own spirit is like a city that is broken down, and without walls" (Prov. 25:28). Self-control guards us against destructive behaviors and fosters a disciplined mind prepared to make discerning choices.

Wellness Points:

1. Daily Declaration: Declare according to Galatians 5:22-23 discernment in your choices.

2. Mindfulness and Gratitude: Practice mindfulness and gratitude daily to enhance emotional resilience.

3. Positive Affirmations: Use positive affirmations to renew your mind and guard against negative thoughts.

4. Prayer and Meditation: Incorporate prayer and meditation to connect with the divine and find peace.

5. Supportive Relationships: Build and maintain relationships that provide emotional and mental support.

Wellness Questions:

1. What steps do you take to nurture your emotional resilience and mental clarity?

   ____

   ____

   ____

2. How do you incorporate gratitude into your daily routine to enhance emotional wellness?

   ____

   ____

   ____

3. What practices help you guard your mind against toxic thoughts?

   ____

   ____

   ____

4. How do you ensure that your mental wellness is supported by your spiritual practices?

   ____

   ____

   ____

5. In what ways do you cultivate supportive relationships that enhance your emotional and mental well-being?

   ____

   ____

   ____

Wellness Notes:

CHAPTER 4:
CREATING SPIRITUAL WELLNESS

Spiritual wellness is the cornerstone of a balanced and fulfilling life. It is about finding peace and purpose, an inner tranquility that transcends daily challenges. To create spiritual wellness, one must connect deeply with their inner self and, in doing so, align with a higher power. This connection paves the way for personal growth and ultimately transforms your entire life.

Connecting with your inner self involves introspection and meditation. This is the time to pause from the hustle and bustle of life and reflect on who you are and what you value. Jesus said, "Come unto me, all ye that labor and are heavy laden, and I will give you rest" (Matt. 11:28). Taking time to rest and reflect can renew your spirit and strengthen your connection to the Divine.

In addition to meditation, prayer plays a crucial role in spiritual wellness. It is a conduit for communication with God, allowing you to express gratitude, seek guidance, and find solace in times of distress. The Apostle Paul encourages us to "Pray without ceasing" (1 Thess. 5:17), highlighting the importance of continual communion with our Creator.

Reading and reflecting upon sacred texts can also deepen your spiritual wellness. The Bible offers timeless wisdom and insights that can help navigate life's complex paths. "Thy word is a lamp unto my feet, and a light unto my path" (Psalm 119:105), serves as a reminder that scripture can guide us through dark and uncertain times.

It is essential to build a supportive community that shares your spiritual values. Surround yourself with like-minded individuals who encourage your growth and hold you accountable. "Wherefore comfort yourselves together, and edify one another, even as also ye do" (1 Thess. 5:11). Fellowship can fortify your faith and provide a network of support.

In your journey toward spiritual wellness, it is equally important to practice gratitude. Recognizing the blessings in your life, both big and small, can cultivate a sense of contentment and joy. Paul reminds us, "In everything give thanks: for this is the will of God in Christ Jesus concerning you" (1 Thess. 5:18). A grateful heart is fertile ground for spiritual growth.

An essential aspect of spiritual wellness is forgiving others, as well as forgiving yourself. Holding onto grudges and past failures can weigh heavily on your spirit, hindering your progress. Jesus taught, "For if ye forgive men their trespasses, your heavenly Father will also forgive you" (Matt. 6:14). Embrace forgiveness as a pathway to emotional and spiritual liberation.

Spiritual wellness is an evolving journey rather than a final destination. It requires consistent effort and dedication. Implementing daily declarations can be a powerful tool in fostering this growth. Declare, "I declare according to Ephesians 1:3 access to spiritual blessings". By speaking these affirmations out loud, you are setting a positive and intentional tone for your spiritual journey.

Life will inevitably present challenges, but spiritual wellness equips you with the resilience to face them. Consider the words of Isaiah, "But they that wait upon the LORD shall renew their strength; they shall mount up with wings as eagles; they shall run, and not be weary; and they shall walk, and not faint" (Isaiah 40:31). Trust in the Lord to be your source of strength and guidance.

Lastly, never underestimate the power of love in cultivating spiritual wellness. Love for yourself, your neighbors, and above all, love for God. "Thou shalt love thy neighbour as thyself" (Matt. 22:39). This love translates into acts of kindness, compassion, and service to others, all of which enrich your spirit.

Love for others, or loving your neighbor as yourself, is central to the teachings of Jesus. In Matthew 22:39, we are commanded, "Thou shalt love thy neighbor as thyself," which reminds us that the way we treat others is a direct reflection of our spiritual maturity. This love is not merely an emotion but an active commitment to kindness, compassion, and understanding toward those around us. It means extending grace to others even when it is difficult, choosing empathy over judgment, and seeking to serve rather than to be served. Acts of kindness, whether small or grand, are powerful expressions of love that deepen our connection to God and to humanity.

Love for God, however, stands at the pinnacle of spiritual wellness. When you love God with all your heart, soul, and mind, as commanded in the Great Commandment (Matthew 22:37), it transforms every aspect of your life. This love manifests in your desire to live according to God's will, in your devotion to prayer and worship, and in your pursuit of a life that reflects God's goodness. Loving God also involves trusting in His plan for your life, surrendering your worries, and finding peace in His presence.

This triad of love—for yourself, for others, and for God—creates a cycle that continuously enriches your spirit. Love for yourself enables you to better love others. As you extend love to others, your spirit grows stronger, and your love for God deepens, because acts of kindness and service to others are expressions of your faith. Every compassionate action, every moment of forgiveness, and every act of service becomes a spiritual practice that nourishes your soul and draws you closer to God.

Creating spiritual wellness is a vital part of living a successful life in wisdom, wealth, and wellness. By aligning with your inner self and the Divine, embracing gratitude and forgiveness, and fostering a loving community, you'll cultivate a profound sense of peace and purpose. Let your spiritual journey be a testament to the transformative power of faith.

In this way, love translates into tangible acts that shape the world around you. Helping a neighbor in need, comforting someone who is hurting, or simply showing patience in difficult moments are all reflections of God's love working through you. These actions not only benefit others but also bring a sense of fulfillment and spiritual wellness to your own life. When you act out of love, you align yourself with God's purpose, allowing His light to shine through you and touch the lives of those around you.

Love, therefore, is the greatest tool for cultivating spiritual wellness. It is through love that we experience the true depth of our connection to God, to ourselves, and to others. This love compels us to serve, to forgive, and to embrace others with the same grace that God has shown us. Ultimately, love enriches our spirit, grounding us in the knowledge that we are part of something greater than ourselves—a divine plan rooted in compassion, grace, and endless love.

Connecting with Your Inner Self

Creating spiritual wellness begins with knowing yourself. Self-awareness is not just about recognizing your strengths and weaknesses but also about connecting with your inner self on a deeper level. This connection forms the bedrock of your spiritual growth and personal development. To truly understand oneself, one must look internally, peeling back the layers that everyday life can add, and engage with the essence of who we truly are.

Your inner self is a reservoir of wisdom and intuition, waiting to be tapped. Nurturing this connection requires time, patience, and consistency. Many find that practices like meditation and prayer serve as powerful tools in this endeavor. These practices allow us to still our minds and listen to our inner voice, free from the distractions of daily life. They open the gateway to divine wisdom, enabling us to hear God's whisper in our hearts.

Jesus often retreated to solitary places to pray, setting an example for us to follow. In Mark 1:35, it's written, "And in the morning, rising up a great while before day, he went out, and departed into a solitary place, and there prayed" (Mark 1:35). This underscores the importance of quiet time with oneself and with God. It is in these moments of solitude that our inner self emerges, and we feel a deeper sense of spiritual connection.

Moreover, connecting with your inner self involves being honest about your feelings, thoughts, and experiences. It is about acknowledging your fears and aspirations, understanding your values, and aligning them with your daily actions. As we engage in this introspective process, we begin to live more authentically, reflecting our true selves in every facet of our lives.

For many, this connection is strengthened through journaling, allowing them to document their thoughts and experiences. By writing down our reflections, we create a tangible record of our inner journey, and it becomes a roadmap to our spiritual wellness. This process of documenting can reveal patterns, breakthroughs, and even divine interventions that we might overlook in the hustle and bustle of daily life.

Additionally, cultivating a strong internal dialogue is beneficial. How we speak to ourselves can influence our spiritual well-being. Positive affirmations, grounded in scripture, help build a resilient inner self. For instance, affirming "I can do all things through Christ which strengtheneth me" (Phil. 4:13) can fortify our inner resolve and remind us of the divine strength that supports us.

Moreover, your connection with your inner self is not a solitary journey. Surrounding yourself with a supportive community that values spiritual wellness can be immensely helpful. Engaging in discussions, sharing experiences, and learning from others can offer new perspectives and insights. It fosters a sense of belonging and strengthens our spiritual resolve as we walk this path together.

Your inner self thrives in an environment of love and respect. Honoring your inner self means honoring the unique gifts and talents you have been given. When we align our actions with our inner truth and spiritual values, we can serve both God and our community in meaningful ways.

Connecting with your inner self is a multidimensional journey that requires intentionality and dedication. It involves introspection, meditation, prayer, journaling, positive self-talk, and community support. As you cultivate this connection, you'll find yourself growing in spiritual wisdom, aligning more closely with God's purpose for your life. Remember, the key to spiritual wellness lies within you, waiting to be unlocked by your authentic engagement and unwavering faith.

Daily Declaration for Spiritual Growth

A Daily Declaration for Spiritual Growth is a conscious commitment to nurturing your spiritual journey, an intentional affirmation of your desire to deepen your relationship with God and align your life with His purpose. This daily practice serves as a reminder of your faith, your reliance on God's strength, and your commitment to walking in His ways. By declaring spiritual truths over your life each day, you reinforce your identity as a child of God and create space for His guidance and presence to shape your actions, thoughts, and emotions.

Beginning each day with such a declaration establishes a sense of purpose and direction. It's a moment where you consciously choose to set your mind and heart on things above, rather than being consumed by the distractions of the world. In this way, your declaration becomes a form of spiritual grounding, a reminder that no matter what happens throughout the day, you are anchored in God's love, truth, and power.

Forgiveness, both given and received, plays a crucial role in spiritual growth, and this can be included in your daily declaration. Declaring, "I choose to forgive others as God has forgiven me," reminds you of the importance of grace and mercy in your interactions. It sets the tone for how you will respond to others, especially when faced with difficult situations or people. This act of forgiveness softens your heart and aligns you with God's command to love your neighbor.

Spiritual growth also requires humility and a continual reliance on God's strength rather than your own. A daily declaration of humility, such as "I acknowledge that apart from God, I can do nothing, but through Him, I can do all things," centers you in the truth that it is God who empowers you to grow, to change, and to overcome. This shift in perspective reminds you that spiritual growth is not solely dependent on your efforts but on God's grace working within you.

I Declare According To Ephesians 1:3 Access To Spiritual Blessings

Creating spiritual wellness in our lives requires intention, consistent effort, and divine wisdom. At the core of this practice is the recognition and declaration of spiritual truths drawn from Scripture. One such powerful affirmation is rooted in Ephesians 1:3, which states, "Blessed be the God and Father of our Lord Jesus Christ, who hath blessed us with all spiritual blessings in heavenly places in Christ" (Ephesians 1:3). This daily declaration can unlock spiritual growth in unprecedented ways and help us access the full spectrum of blessings that God has prepared for us.

The first step in cultivating spiritual wellness is the understanding that we are already blessed with every spiritual blessing through our relationship with Christ. This is not something we need to earn or strive for; it has already been given to us by God through Jesus. These blessings are not material or worldly but spiritual in nature, meaning they are eternal, transformative, and available to us in every aspect of our lives. By recognizing this truth and declaring it daily, we begin to align ourselves with the fullness of what God has intended for us.

Secondly, when we make the daily declaration that God has already blessed us with all spiritual blessings in Christ, we unlock the potential for spiritual growth in unprecedented ways. This affirmation serves as a reminder that we are not lacking anything spiritually; we have access to all the resources we need to grow in faith, wisdom, love, and spiritual understanding. It shifts our mindset from one of scarcity or striving to one of abundance and gratitude, knowing that God has equipped us with everything necessary to live a life of spiritual richness and fulfillment.

Accessing these blessings, however, requires intentionality and consistent effort on our part. It is one thing to declare that we are blessed, but another to actively seek to understand and utilize these blessings in our daily lives. This means engaging in spiritual practices such as prayer, studying Scripture, worship, and service to others. These practices create space for us to receive and experience the blessings God has already provided. They open our hearts and minds to the deeper truths of God's Word and help us grow in our understanding of His love, grace, and purpose for our lives.

In the third step, this daily declaration invites us to live with a sense of expectancy and faith. When we affirm that we are blessed with all spiritual blessings, we position ourselves to expect and recognize the work of God in our lives. It encourages us to approach each day with the confidence that God is working in and through us, even in situations that may seem difficult or overwhelming. This shift in perspective helps us see challenges as opportunities for growth and transformation, trusting that God's spiritual blessings are at work in every circumstance.

The act of declaring, "I declare according to Ephesians 1:3 access to spiritual blessings," is more than mere words. It's a profound affirmation of faith that aligns our spirit with God's promises. By consistently affirming this, we remind ourselves and the spiritual realm that we are recipients of divine blessings. When we speak words of faith, we set in motion the spiritual forces needed to bring those declarations to fruition.

Spiritual blessings extend beyond the physical realm. While material blessings are visible and often tangible, spiritual blessings are the unseen forces that shape our lives. These include peace, wisdom, joy, love, and an intimate relationship with God. Imagine starting your day with the conscious awareness that you have access to these heavenly treasures. It transforms your perspective, fills you with hope, and sets a positive tone for the rest of your day.

The declaration based on Ephesians 1:3 also fosters a deeper connection with our inner selves. It prompts reflection and gratitude, reminding us of the spiritual assets we often overlook. When confronted with life's challenges, we can draw strength from the knowledge that we are blessed with spiritual resources far more potent than any adversity. This sense of inner abundance enables us to approach difficulties not with a spirit of defeat but with an attitude of victory.

Moreover, understanding and accessing these spiritual blessings can significantly enhance our ability to serve others. When we're conscious of the love, joy, and peace we've received, it becomes natural to extend these blessings to those around us. Acts of kindness, words of encouragement, and selfless service flow more freely from hearts that are spiritually enriched. By declaring our access to spiritual blessings, we open ourselves to be conduits of God's love and grace to the world.

In addition to enabling service to others, spiritual blessings also fortify our emotional and mental health. The peace of God, which transcends all understanding, guards our hearts and minds in Christ Jesus (Philippians 4:7). Joy in the Lord becomes our strength (Nehemiah 8:10), and divine wisdom guides our decisions and actions (James 1:5). These blessings serve as an anchor for our souls, providing stability and resilience amid life's storms.

The process of daily declarations is also an exercise in building spiritual discipline. Just as physical exercise strengthens the body over time, spiritual declarations fortify our faith and spiritual muscles. Repetition is key. The more we affirm God's truths over our lives, the more these truths become integrated into our consciousness. They shape our identity, influence our actions, and ultimately mold our destiny.

It's essential to personalize this declaration, making it a reflection of your unique spiritual journey. As you declare, "I declare according to Ephesians 1:3 access to spiritual blessings," visualize the specific aspects of your life where you seek God's blessings. Whether it's wisdom for making decisions, peace amid chaos, or joy during trying times, name these blessings and envision their manifestation in your life. This imaginative engagement reinforces the power of your declaration and aligns your expectations with God's promises.

Our daily declaration for spiritual growth, rooted in Ephesians 1:3, is a powerful tool for accessing the full scope of God's blessings. It aligns us with divine truth, strengthens our faith, and empowers us to live out our spiritual potential. By consistently declaring this truth, we invite God's presence into our lives and position ourselves to receive The Lord's abundant blessings.

Wellness Points:

1. Daily Declaration: Declare according to Ephesians 1:3 access to spiritual blessings.

2. Meditation and Reflection: Engage in regular meditation and reflection to connect with your inner self.

3. Prayer Practice: Establish a consistent prayer practice to seek guidance and express gratitude.

4. Scriptural Study: Study and reflect on scriptures to deepen your spiritual understanding and growth.

5. Community Support: Participate in a supportive community that shares your spiritual values.

Wellness Questions:

1. How do you connect with your inner self to enhance your spiritual wellness?

    ____

    ____

    ____

2. What role does prayer play in your daily spiritual practice?

    ____

    ____

    ____

3. How do you incorporate forgiveness into your spiritual journey?

    ____

    ____

    ____

4. In what ways do you build a supportive spiritual community?

    ____

    ____

    ____

5. How do you use scripture to guide your spiritual growth and well-being?

    ____

    ____

    ____

Wellness Notes:

Chapter 5:
Building Wealth Through Declarations

Wealth creation often seems like a mysterious endeavor, reserved only for a select few. However, the scriptures reveal that abundance is accessible to every believer who aligns their thoughts and words with God's promises. The foundation of this mindset lies in the power of declarations. James 1:17 tells us that "Every good gift and every perfect gift is from above, and cometh down from the Father of lights" (James 1:17). Recognizing that our source of wealth is divine is the first step toward manifesting it in our lives.

Let's begin by examining the mindset of wealth. The world often views wealth through the lens of material accumulation, but biblical wealth encompasses much more. True prosperity includes health, relationships, and a sense of purpose. Thus, wealth should not bring stress and anxiety; instead, it should be accompanied by peace and joy.

Next, we'll delve into how daily declarations can transform not just your bank account, but your entire outlook on life. Declaring God's promises over your life daily shifts your mindset from scarcity to abundance. By speaking words of prosperity, you align yourself with God's plans, propelling yourself towards financial abundance.

Let's put this into practical terms. Think about people who consistently succeed in their financial endeavors. They possess a certain confidence and optimism that seems unshakeable. This isn't mere luck or talent; it's the result of continuously declaring positive outcomes and believing in their success. Joshua 1:8 instructs us, "This book of the law shall not depart out of thy mouth; but thou shalt meditate therein day and night" (Joshua 1:8). Meditating on God's Word doesn't just mean silent reflection; it involves speaking it into existence.

Declaring financial abundance over your life isn't a one-time event; it's a daily practice. Such a practice sets the tone for your day and creates an atmosphere of expectancy and faith. Repetition not only helps to solidify these truths in your heart but also reinforces them in your subconscious mind.

It's crucial to understand that wealth declarations aren't just about acquiring money. They're about recognizing and appreciating the multifaceted richness that God offers. Whether it's an unexpectedly good health report, a serendipitous business opportunity, or the strengthening of personal relationships, these are all manifestations of God's abundant gifts.

Exploring the power of declarations shouldn't stop here. Make it a part of your family's daily practices. Encourage loved ones to declare positive outcomes in their lives. This collective practice will build a culture of faith and abundance in your household, further amplifying the impact of your declarations.

Reflect on how you can integrate financial declarations into your daily life. Make them a consistent part of your routine, just as you do with prayer and meditation. Begin today with the declaration: "I declare according to James 1:17 that I receive greatness and prosperity because every good and perfect gift comes from the Father of lights."

The Mindset of Wealth

When we talk about building wealth through declarations, it's crucial to address the mindset that underpins such a journey. To foster financial abundance, you need to cultivate a mindset of wealth. This is not merely about the accumulation of money but involves a broader perspective on abundance, gratitude, and stewardship. A wealth mindset acts as fertile soil where your seeds of declarations can take root and flourish.

The Bible says, "For as he thinketh in his heart, so is he" (Prov. 23:7). This scripture underscores the profound impact that our inner beliefs and attitudes have on our outward realities. A mindset grounded in scarcity will see lack in every corner, missing opportunities and potential for growth. By contrast, a mindset of abundance acknowledges God as a plentitude, the source of all good things, paving the way for prosperity and peace.

First and foremost, one must recognize that wealth is not an end but a means—a tool to fulfill God's purpose in your life. We are too prioritize our spiritual values over material obsession. Wealth is a tool for service, not a master to serve. When your heart is aligned with divine purposes, wealth becomes a byproduct of a life lived righteously and wisely.

A wealthy mindset is characterized by faith and expectation. Your declarations are fuelled by faith—believing in the unseen and expecting God to honor The Lord's promises. When you declare financial abundance, it's not wishful thinking but an act of aligning yourself with God's promises and providence.

The road to building wealth also involves honoring the principles of hard work and diligence. While declarations help you set the stage, diligence and effort are essential to bring those declarations to fruition. Laziness and complacency have no place in a wealth-building journey.

Furthermore, adopting a mindset of stewardship rather than ownership is pivotal. Recognizing that everything you have belongs to God changes your approach to wealth. It becomes less about accumulating and more about managing resources responsibly to honor God and contribute to The Lord's kingdom.

A mindset of wealth involves continuous learning and growth. The journey to financial abundance isn't static but dynamic, requiring you to continually seek knowledge and adapt. By staying curious and open-minded, you position yourself to recognize and seize divine opportunities.

Embracing a wealth mindset also means trusting in God's timing and provision. There may be periods of waiting and preparation, which are essential for refining your character and expanding your capacity for the blessings to come. Trusting in God's timing prevents you from making hasty, fear-driven decisions that could jeopardize your financial well-being.

Lastly, a wealth mindset celebrates success, both yours and others'. When you celebrate others' successes, you create an atmosphere of positivity and expectation. The energy of celebration amplifies your own blessings and opens doors for further prosperity. Envy and resentment, on the other hand, block your blessings and foster a mentality of lack.

In conclusion, cultivating a wealth mindset is foundational for building wealth through declarations. It aligns your thoughts, attitudes, and actions with divine principles and promises, ensuring that your journey towards financial abundance is not only successful but also purposeful. With faith, diligence, gratitude, and a heart for godly stewardship, you set the stage for a prosperous and fulfilling life.

Daily Declaration for Financial Abundance

A Daily Declaration for Financial Abundance is a powerful tool that helps shift your mindset toward gratitude, responsibility, and trust in God's provision. It is not merely a statement of desire for wealth, but a purposeful affirmation that recognizes God as the ultimate source of all resources and blessings. By making this declaration each day, you align your thoughts, actions, and financial decisions with the principles of stewardship and faith.

Starting your day with a declaration focused on financial abundance reminds you that God is the provider of all your needs. It reinforces the truth found in scriptures like Philippians 4:19, which says, "And my God will meet all your needs according to the riches of his glory in Christ Jesus." This declaration is not just about asking for financial wealth, but about acknowledging that God is sufficient to meet every need, whether material, emotional, or spiritual. It helps you cultivate an attitude of trust, removing the fear and anxiety that can often accompany financial concerns.

Declaring financial abundance also positions you to be a good steward of what you have been entrusted with. It encourages you to manage your resources wisely, knowing that what you have, no matter the amount, is a blessing from God. When you affirm daily that you are capable of making sound financial decisions, you strengthen your resolve to budget, save, and invest responsibly. This declaration also fosters a heart of generosity, reminding you that financial abundance is not just for personal gain but to be used in service to others and in furthering God's kingdom.

This practice further emphasizes gratitude. When you declare financial abundance, you are not simply focusing on what you want or lack, but on the blessings you already possess. Gratitude opens the door for greater peace and contentment in your financial life. By recognizing the small and large ways in which God has already provided, you shift your mindset from scarcity to abundance, understanding that God is faithful and will continue to meet your needs in the future.

Another key aspect of this declaration is the focus on faith and patience. Financial abundance does not always mean immediate wealth or material prosperity. Instead, it reflects the long-term blessings that come from trusting in God's timing and provision. By affirming that financial abundance is yours in Christ, you release the need for control and allow God to work in your life according to His divine timing. This teaches patience and trust, knowing that God's plan for your financial life may unfold in ways you cannot yet see.

In conclusion, a Daily Declaration for Financial Abundance is a holistic practice that grounds your financial life in trust, stewardship, gratitude, and faith. It invites God's provision into your finances while reminding you of your role as a faithful steward of His blessings. By consistently affirming these truths, you can foster a healthy relationship with money, reduce financial anxiety, and live with a sense of abundance that transcends material wealth, focusing instead on the fullness of life that God promises.

I Declare According to James 1:17 Greatness and Prosperity

As we journey into the realm of financial abundance, it's crucial to anchor ourselves in solid, faith-driven declarations. The words we speak carry immense power, shaping the reality we experience and the future we wish to create. James 1:17 tells us, "Every good gift and every perfect gift is from above, and cometh down from the Father of lights, with whom is no variableness, neither shadow of turning" (James 1:17). This scripture serves as a foundation for our declaration of greatness and prosperity, reminding us that true wealth and blessings come from a steadfast and generous God.

Building wealth is not merely about accumulating material possessions or money. It's about recognizing and harnessing the blessings that God has already poured into our lives. By acknowledging that every good thing in our lives is a gift from above, we align ourselves with a higher purpose and a divine plan. This mindset shift can dramatically influence our approach to wealth, leading us to pursue prosperity not just for personal gain, but for the broader impact it can have in the world.

When we declare greatness and prosperity according to James 1:17, we're proclaiming that our financial well-being is governed by divine principles. This declaration isn't just a casual affirmation but a powerful, faith-filled statement that shifts our mentality. We're stepping into a space where we recognize that God's gifts are perfect and that The Lord's provision is unending. By doing so, we position ourselves to receive financial abundance that extends beyond the limits of human understanding.

One of the key aspects of this declaration is understanding the nature of God's gifts. Unlike worldly wealth which can be transient and fluctuating, the blessings from God are consistent and enduring.

This constancy is described in James 1:17, which highlights that with God, there is "no variableness, neither shadow of turning." This emphasizes the reliability and permanence of divine blessings, offering us a source of unshakeable confidence as we seek financial prosperity.

The declaration for financial abundance involves more than just faith; it also requires action. By recognizing that every good and perfect gift is from above, we are called to be stewards of these gifts. Stewardship involves managing our resources wisely, investing with discernment, and giving generously. It is through such acts that we honor the sources of our blessings and ensure that our wealth is used to further God's kingdom.

Applying this declaration in our daily lives means infusing our financial decisions with wisdom and integrity. Are we making choices that reflect our faith and values? Are we seeking guidance from God in our investment and spending decisions? By constantly aligning our financial practices with the divine principles in James 1:17, we reinforce our commitment to a life of true prosperity. This declaration serves as a reminder to remain grateful. Gratitude shifts our focus from what we lack to what we have been blessed with. It cultivates a sense of contentment and joy that's independent of our financial status. When we start each day declaring greatness and prosperity according to James 1:17, we open our hearts to recognize and appreciate the blessings God has already bestowed upon us.

Expanding this declaration to encompass not just personal but communal prosperity is vital. As we thrive, let's strive to uplift others. Financial abundance isn't solely a personal accomplishment; it's an opportunity to create a ripple effect of generosity and support. Hebrews 13:16 advises us, "But to do good and to communicate forget not: for with such sacrifices God is well pleased" (Heb. 13:16). By sharing our blessings, we engage in a larger divine economy where wealth circulates, benefiting all.

Lastly, it's essential to remain grounded in humility. We must recognize that the source of our greatness and prosperity is God alone. Arrogance and pride can derail the blessings we've received. By continually affirming that every good and perfect gift is from above, we keep our hearts humble and our spirits teachable, which in turn keeps the channels of divine blessings open.

This declaration is a potent tool for transforming our lives. It's a daily reminder that our financial well-being is rooted in divine provision and guided by heavenly wisdom. As we declare according to James 1:17 greatness and prosperity, we embrace a holistic understanding of wealth, one that transcends material gain and encompasses spiritual richness, emotional fulfillment, and communal well-being.

Remember, the power of our words, backed by the timeless truth of scripture, has the capability to unlock doors of prosperity and greatness beyond our wildest imaginations.

Wellness Points:

1. Daily Declaration: Declare according to James 1:17 greatness and prosperity.

2. Financial Stewardship: Practice responsible financial stewardship, recognizing wealth as a tool for greater good.

3. Generosity: Cultivate generosity, using your resources to bless others and further your mission.

4. Gratitude for Wealth: Maintain a mindset of gratitude for all forms of wealth, both material and spiritual.

5. Purpose-Driven Wealth: Align your financial goals with your divine purpose and long-term vision.

Wellness Questions:

1. How do you redefine wealth to include both material and spiritual abundance?

    ____

    ____

    ____

2. What steps do you take to ensure your financial practices align with your spiritual values?

    ____

    ____

    ____

3. How do you cultivate a mindset of gratitude and generosity in relation to wealth?

    ____

    ____

    ____

4. In what ways do you use your financial resources to support your divine mission?

    ____

    ____

    ____

5. How do you balance the pursuit of financial stability with your overall well-being?

    ____

    ____

    ____

Wellness Notes:

CHAPTER 6:
ACHIEVING GENERATIONAL WEALTH

The concept of generational wealth isn't just about amassing money. It's about building a legacy that allows your children, and their children, to start on higher ground financially. Proverbs 13:22 tells us, "A good man leaveth an inheritance to his children's children" (Prov. 13:22). Think about that. We're not merely talking about our immediate offspring but extending our vision further down the timeline.

Generational wealth is not limited to material assets like money, property, or businesses. It also includes passing down knowledge, values, and the wisdom required to manage and grow those resources. By teaching our children financial literacy, responsibility, and the importance of stewardship, we equip them with the tools they need to sustain and build upon what is left to them. This form of wealth transcends mere dollars and cents; it prepares future generations to thrive, not only economically but also in terms of character and discipline.

Building generational wealth involves creating a financial foundation that allows future generations to avoid the struggles of starting from nothing or from a place of financial instability. Instead, they can begin their lives with a solid base from which to pursue education, entrepreneurship, or other opportunities that create further growth. It's about giving them the freedom to make choices that are not solely dictated by financial necessity, but driven by passion, purpose, and calling.

Why is generational wealth significant? First, it provides a buffer against life's inevitable hardships. Imagine your descendants having the luxury not to worry about student loans, or being able to start a business without the stranglehold of debt. More than money, though, it's the practices and mindsets that are equally important to pass down. Financial literacy, wise investments, and an understanding of the power of compound interest can transform lives.

But let's be clear: achieving this kind of wealth takes intentionality. It involves strategic planning and a disciplined approach to saving and investing. It's in these moments we look to scriptures for guidance. Take Deuteronomy 28:3-4, "Blessed shalt thou be in the city, and blessed shalt thou be in the field. Blessed shall be the fruit of thy body, and the fruit of thy ground, and the fruit of thy cattle, the increase of thy kine, and the flocks of thy sheep" (Deut. 28:3-4). This scripture reminds us that God wants us to prosper in all aspects of our lives.

Next, we need to talk about financial freedom. True financial freedom isn't just having a lot of money; it's having enough to live comfortably and provide for future generations without burden. It's about proclaiming liberation from the chains of financial worry. This requires both education and action. Understanding investment vehicles like stocks, bonds, and real estate is crucial. Moreover, passing on the knowledge is as important as passing on the wealth itself.

Creating trusts, wisely allocating assets, and having a comprehensive estate plan matter immensely. These aren't just tools for the wealthy; they're tools for anyone aiming to leave a financial footprint in the sand for others to follow. The advantage of beginning these processes early can't be overstated.

Daily declarations can serve as a compass guiding us towards this vision. "I declare according to Deuteronomy 28:3-4 generational blessings," can be a powerful affirmation. Words have power, forming the bedrock of our actions. Speak positivity and prosperity over your endeavors and let those declarations shape your reality.

Additionally, the journey isn't just financial but spiritual and emotional. The fruits of the spirit mentioned in Galatians remind us to cultivate love, joy, peace, patience, kindness, goodness, faithfulness, gentleness, and self-control in our financial habits. There's wisdom in knowing when to sow and when to reap, guided by prudence and Divine wisdom.

In moments of doubt, remember the story of Joseph. He interpreted dreams that led Egypt to prepare for seven years of famine during seven years of abundance (Gen. 41:28-30). Like Joseph, foresight can save future generations from calamities. If we store up not just wealth, but wisdom and spiritual guidance, our family will thrive even in uncertain times.

Kicking off this journey might seem daunting. However, remember that each small step, each prayerful deed, contributes to the bigger picture. Invoke the strength and provision Divinely ordained for prosperity. "The LORD shall command the blessing upon thee in thy storehouses, and in all that thou settest thine hand unto" (Deut. 28:8). Ground your plans in faith, diligently work towards them, and rest in the assurance that you're working not just for temporal gain but an everlasting impact.

Finally, let's circle back to the community. Generational wealth isn't solely a personal mission; it can and should extend to community uplift. As you build your wealth, consider ways to lift others. Whether through mentorship, educational programs, or charitable endeavors, enrich the community and create a ripple effect of success.

The Importance of Financial Freedom

The journey to achieving generational wealth is profoundly tied to the concept of financial freedom. Financial freedom isn't merely a buzzword; it's a powerful cornerstone in the edifice of wealth that can be passed down through generations. It allows you to make choices that align with your values and long-term goals, free from the anxieties that accompany financial constraints. As Proverbs 22:7 tells us, "The rich ruleth over the poor, and the borrower is servant to the lender" (Prov. 22:7). This Biblical wisdom underscores the significance of financial independence and how it sets the stage for a more empowered life.

At its core, financial freedom means that you have achieved a state where your financial resources are no longer solely dedicated to meeting basic needs or managing debt. Instead, you have the ability to invest, save, and allocate your wealth toward meaningful goals that reflect your values—whether that involves providing for your children's education, investing in property, starting a business, or contributing to charitable causes. This autonomy enables individuals to make decisions based on long-term benefits rather than short-term survival, which is key to building a legacy of wealth.

Achieving financial freedom allows you to think strategically about your financial future and the future of your family. Without the anxiety that accompanies financial constraints, you are empowered to make thoughtful decisions about how to grow and protect your wealth. This might include making investments that appreciate over time, setting up trust funds for your children, or ensuring that your assets are properly managed and safeguarded for the future. It also gives you the freedom to take calculated risks that can lead to greater financial opportunities, knowing that you have a solid foundation in place.

Consider, for a moment, the myriad opportunities that emerge when you're not shackled by debt or living paycheck to paycheck. Financial freedom opens doors to invest in education, pursue entrepreneurial ventures, and, perhaps most importantly, to give generously. Having the means to support not only your immediate family but also to leave a legacy for future generations is a transformative blessing.

Financial freedom also offers the liberty to live a life of purpose and a higher calling. When you aren't pressured to meet basic needs, your mind is free to focus on fostering talents, building meaningful relationships, and contributing to society in impactful ways. For example, the ability to volunteer your time or donate to causes that matter can significantly enhance your spiritual and emotional well-being. Moreover, it allows you to act with integrity, aligning your financial decisions with your ethical and moral principles.

Looking through a broader lens, achieving financial independence creates a ripple effect that extends far beyond personal benefits. It strengthens community ties and enhances societal welfare. Financially secure individuals can support local businesses, contribute to philanthropic endeavors, and advocate for social justice. The Bible encourages us to be stewards of our blessings: "For unto whomsoever much is given, of him shall be much required" (Luke 12:48). By achieving financial freedom, we equip ourselves to fulfill this divine responsibility.

Yet, financial freedom isn't only about accumulation; it's deeply tied to stewardship and wise management of resources. We are called to be prudent managers of what God has entrusted to us. In the parable of the talents, Jesus highlights the importance of investing and growing what we have been given. Scripture reminds us that responsible financial stewardship is key to unlocking greater opportunities and blessings.

Financial freedom provides a sense of security that guards against life's uncertainties. Emergencies, health issues, and unexpected expenses can wreak havoc on someone who's financially unprepared. The peace of mind that comes with having a financial cushion allows you not only to navigate these challenges more effectively but to do so with grace and confidence.

Another critical dimension of financial freedom is the ability to invest in future generations. By laying down a solid financial foundation, you provide your descendants with opportunities that may have been out of reach. This not only includes monetary wealth but also the education, values, and wisdom needed to manage those resources effectively. As previously mentioned, Proverbs 13:22 states, "A good man leaveth an inheritance to his children's children," emphasizing the importance of thinking long-term and beyond one's immediate circumstances.

In a more practical sense, financial freedom empowers you to seize life's opportunities when they arise. Whether it's a unique investment opportunity, a chance to travel and learn from different cultures, or the ability to spend quality time with loved ones, having the financial resources to act on these opportunities enriches your life's tapestry.

Finally, the pursuit of financial freedom encourages a disciplined, intentional approach to life. It requires diligent planning, consistent effort, and a mindset that values delayed gratification over immediate pleasures. The financial habits you cultivate in this quest are beneficial not just for accumulating wealth, but also in fostering a life of discipline and purpose. It empowers you to live a life of purpose, become a steward of God's blessings, and prepare a legacy for your descendants. Through prudent financial management and a heart aligned with divine wisdom, you pave the way for a future where prosperity and abundance are not just dreams but lived realities for generations to come.

Daily Declaration for Building Wealth

A Daily Declaration for Building Wealth is a powerful practice that combines intention, faith, and action to cultivate a mindset focused on financial growth and stewardship. It is more than just speaking positive words; it is about aligning your beliefs, thoughts, and actions with the principles that foster true wealth-building. By making a declaration each day, you affirm your commitment to the process of creating wealth in a way that reflects integrity, diligence, and trust in God's provision.

At the core of a daily wealth-building declaration is the recognition that wealth is not solely about acquiring money, but about cultivating a life of abundance that encompasses financial security, personal growth, and the ability to positively impact others. When you declare daily, "I am building wealth with wisdom, discipline, and faith," you remind yourself of the values that undergird true wealth. This affirmation helps you maintain focus on the long-term process, emphasizing consistent actions like budgeting, saving, investing, and making wise financial decisions.

A daily declaration also strengthens your belief in your ability to create wealth. Often, our mindset can be the greatest obstacle to financial growth. Thoughts of lack, scarcity, or fear of failure can prevent us from fully embracing opportunities for wealth creation. By declaring daily that you are capable of building wealth, you counter these negative beliefs and replace them with a mindset of abundance and possibility. Statements like, "I am open to new financial opportunities, and I trust in my ability to manage and grow my resources," help to shift your perspective and cultivate confidence in your financial journey.

In addition to personal empowerment, these declarations invite a sense of responsibility and stewardship over the resources you have.

Wealth-building is not just about accumulation but also about managing what you have with care and wisdom. A daily declaration can serve as a reminder to approach your finances with discipline, ensuring that every decision is made with a view toward long-term growth and sustainability. Declarations such as, "I am a faithful steward of my finances, and I use my resources wisely," reinforce the importance of diligence and responsibility in wealth-building.

Faith plays a crucial role in the process of building wealth. For those who view wealth through a spiritual lens, daily declarations can also involve trusting in God's provision and timing. Affirming that "God is my provider, and He blesses the work of my hands" shifts the focus from self-reliance to divine guidance. This trust allows you to work diligently without anxiety, knowing that your efforts are supported by a higher purpose and that abundance is a result of both faith and action.

Lastly, a daily declaration for building wealth emphasizes the purpose of wealth beyond personal gain. By declaring, "I build wealth to create a legacy and to bless others," you align your financial goals with a greater sense of mission. Wealth is not just for personal comfort or security but can be used as a tool to help others, to give back, and to contribute to causes that matter. This broader perspective encourages generosity and positions wealth-building as a way to serve both your family and the wider community.

I Declare According To Deuteronomy 28: 3-4 Generational Blessings

Building generational wealth isn't merely about financial investments or accumulating material possessions; it's about creating a legacy that transcends time. "Blessed shalt thou be in the city, and blessed shalt thou be in the field. Blessed shall be the fruit of thy body, and the fruit of thy ground, and the fruit of thy cattle, the increase of thy kine, and the flocks of thy sheep" (Deut. 28:3-4). This powerful scripture provides a divine vision for passing down blessings from one generation to another.

Generational wealth is conceived with the understanding that God's blessings aren't confined to one point in time but are meant to ripple throughout generations. By invoking Deuteronomy 28:3-4 in our daily declarations, we're not only speaking prosperity into existence for ourselves but for our descendants. Wealth that stems from divine blessings incorporates spiritual, emotional, and financial abundance. It aligns us with a holistic perspective on wealth, ensuring that our legacy isn't just rich in dollars but rich in spiritual and moral fiber.

When we embrace these declarations, we set a precedent. Each word reinforces a mindset and behavior conducive to long-lasting prosperity and well-being. These declarations have a profound impact on how we approach daily decisions and challenges. They remind us of a higher purpose, a grander goal beyond immediate gratification. Our daily practices, guided by this scripture, cultivate a culture of diligence, integrity, and wisdom, vital for nurturing generational wealth.

Considering the deeper meaning of Deuteronomy 28:3-4, we realize that generational blessings involve more than just prosperity — they are about holistic growth. Our families become fertile ground just as the scripture describes: fruitful in body, work, and material gain.

This fertility touches all spheres of life, ensuring that our descendants inherit not only financial resources but also the values and wisdom necessary to manage and grow that wealth.

Let's delve deeper into what these declarations can look like in practical terms. For many of us, daily declarations are spoken affirmations. By declaring "I am blessed in the city and the field; my offspring are blessed, and all my endeavors bear fruit," we align ourselves with God's promise. This act of faith transforms our mindset. Moreover, hearing and speaking these words daily instill a constant reminder that our actions are stepping stones toward a prosperous legacy.

Our blessings aren't limited to wealth but extend to the well-being of our families, the success of our ventures, and the richness of our spiritual lives. When our hearts are focused on Deuteronomy 28:3-4, we adopt an attitude of expectancy. We look for opportunities to prosper and thrive, conscious that each effort contributes to a greater, divine purpose.

In the hustle to build wealth, it's easy to lose sight of the moral and ethical dimensions. However, by declaring God's promises over our lives, we maintain a balanced approach. Our endeavors are blessed because they are grounded in righteousness, not just worldly ambition. Declarations based on God's word ensure that our wealth-building strategies are ethically sound and aligned with divine principles.

In every financial decision, we see God's hand at work. From investments to career choices, everything is touched by the assurance that we and our descendants are blessed. This divine assurance fosters patience and resilience. When challenges arise, our faith in God's promises gives us the strength to persevere, knowing that setbacks are temporary and part of the broader journey to generational wealth. These declarations enhance how we pass on wisdom to our descendants. Teaching them to rely on God's blessings nurtures emotional and spiritual maturity. They learn to see wealth not just as material accumulation but as divine stewardship. This insight is the cornerstone of true generational wealth, transforming financial knowledge into a holistic life philosophy.

To wrap this up, consider how Deuteronomy 28:3-4 enriches our understanding of wealth and generational blessings. These verses invite us to see prosperity as all-encompassing, reaching every facet of life. By declaring this scripture daily, we're not only affirming our present circumstances but also planting seeds for future generations to harvest. As we meditate on these promises, we solidify a legacy of wisdom, moral integrity, and divine favor – the true essence of generational wealth.

Deuteronomy 28:3-4 paints a picture of wealth and blessings that extend far beyond mere financial gain. These verses emphasize that true prosperity encompasses every aspect of life, including health, relationships, work, and spiritual well-being. By embracing this holistic view of prosperity, we understand that God's blessings are designed to touch all areas of our lives, bringing fullness and abundance in every dimension.

Wellness Points:

1. Daily Declaration: Declare according to Deuteronomy 28:3-4 generational blessings.

2. Financial Education: Invest in financial education for yourself and your family to build a strong foundation.

3. Long-term Planning: Create a comprehensive financial plan that includes saving, investing, and estate planning.

4. Wise Stewardship: Practice wise stewardship, recognizing that your wealth is meant to benefit future generations.

5. Biblical Principles: Incorporate biblical principles of generosity, stewardship, and faith into your financial practices.

Wellness Questions:

1. What legacy do you want to leave for future generations, both financially and spiritually?

   ____

   ____

   ____

2. How can you educate your family about financial literacy and wise stewardship?

   ____

   ____

   ____

3. What steps can you take today to start building generational wealth?

   ____

   ____

   ____

4. How do you balance immediate financial needs with long-term wealth-building goals?

   ____

   ____

   ____

5. In what ways can you incorporate biblical principles into your financial planning for future generations?

   ____

   ____

   ____

Wellness Notes:

Chapter 7:
Cultural Perspective on Provision

In many cultures around the world, the concept of provision is tied intricately to the idea of a higher power providing for our daily needs. This deep-seated belief often influences how people manage their resources, interact with their community, and approach life's challenges. It's crucial to understand that the cultural lens through which we view provision affects our mindset, decisions, and ultimately, our destinies.

This belief in divine provision influences how people manage their resources, often encouraging a mindset of stewardship rather than ownership. When individuals believe that what they have—whether it's money, food, or other material possessions—comes from a higher source, they may feel a responsibility to manage those resources wisely. In cultures with this outlook, there is often a greater emphasis on sharing and generosity, since resources are viewed not as something hoarded for personal gain but as blessings meant to be distributed for the common good. This shapes decisions on how wealth is accumulated, saved, or shared, and often leads to practices of charity and support within families and communities.

This cultural view of provision also affects how people approach life's challenges. In times of hardship, the belief that a higher power will provide can instill a sense of hope and resilience. When individuals face financial struggles, food scarcity, or other difficulties, their faith in divine provision can offer them emotional strength and a sense of purpose, allowing them to continue working through their challenges with the belief that their needs will be met. This mindset contrasts with a purely self-reliant perspective, which may lead to feelings of isolation or despair when resources run thin.

The cultural lens of provision impacts one's long-term mindset and decision-making. In many cultures, this belief encourages a focus on long-term well-being, understanding that life's abundance is often cyclical and that trusting in divine timing is key. People raised with this belief may approach financial decisions with patience and a broader perspective, knowing that provision may not always come in immediate or expected forms, but will arrive nonetheless. It fosters a spirit of contentment, where one is grateful for what they have and remains open to future blessings, rather than being driven by fear or scarcity.

One's cultural background can shape attitudes towards hard work, charity, and community support. For example, in many cultures, there's a strong emphasis on communal living and shared resources. People believe that blessings multiply when shared. This perspective shifts the focus from individual accumulation to collective well-being. "Give, and it shall be given unto you," as Luke 6:38 (KJV) states, underscores the principle that generosity begets abundance.

However, it's essential to couple cultural practices with the wisdom found in Scriptures. Cultures that emphasize dependency on divine provision generally instill a sense of peace and security among their people. This is especially important in times of scarcity or uncertainty. Proverbs 3:5 (KJV) advises, "Trust in the LORD with all thine heart; and lean not unto thine own understanding." This suggests that cultivating a mindset of dependency on God transcends cultural boundaries and finds universal application.

It's not uncommon for cultures to intertwine their traditional practices with their beliefs about divine provision. Whether it's through the rituals, festivals, or daily prayers, recognizing a higher power in control fosters a sense of gratitude. Living with this perspective aligns well with the Biblical instruction: "But my God shall supply all your need according to his riches in glory by Christ Jesus" (Phil. 4:19, KJV).

From a Biblical standpoint, the idea of provision encompasses both spiritual and material abundance. When Jesus taught his disciples to pray, He included the line, "Give us this day our daily bread" (Matt. 6:11, KJV). This mirrors the daily reliance on God's generosity and opens our hearts to recognize the daily blessings bestowed upon us.

Adopting a Biblical perspective on provision encourages us to look beyond our immediate circumstances and trust in a providential plan that transcends human understanding. It shifts our focus from scarcity to abundance and transforms our attitude towards wealth and resources. Trusting in God's provision allows us to be generous without fear of lack, fostering a community where everyone flourishes.

It is vital to attach our faith to practical actions. Cultures that exemplify this balance tend to thrive not because they have an abundance of resources, but because they have an abundance of faith. This is echoed in 2 Corinthians 9:8 (KJV), "And God is able to make all grace abound toward you; that ye, always having all sufficiency in all things, may abound to every good work."

Let's acknowledge that while culture indeed influences our perception of provision, our ultimate trust must be in God. This is the daily declaration for trusting in generosity, based on Philippians 4:19: "I Declare According to Philippians 4:19 Daily Provisions." This declaration underscores that our provision comes from a higher source, one that never dries up or runs out.

Cultivating a Mindset of Dependency on God

In our quest for success, the notion of provision takes a central stage. While modern culture often equates provision with self-sufficiency, true provision in a Biblical sense goes much deeper. It necessitates a deliberate mindset of dependency on God. Understanding that God's provision is not just about material wealth, but about daily sustenance and spiritual fulfillment, is crucial for thriving both in good times and in challenging seasons.

Consider the words of Jesus in the Sermon on the Mount: "But seek ye first the kingdom of God, and his righteousness; and all these things shall be added unto you" (Matt. 6:33). These words challenge the self-reliance so prevalent in today's world, urging us to lean into God's provision instead. This perspective reshuffles our priorities, placing a firm emphasis on spiritual wealth that, in turn, influences our material well-being.

Cultivating a dependency on God requires us to continually reframe our understanding of daily needs. It's tempting to rely solely on our abilities or the safety net of our social structures, but true faith encourages us to acknowledge God as our ultimate provider. It means confiding in The Lord not only during our scarcity but also in our abundance. By consistently turning to God for guidance and provision, we reinforce our spiritual reliance, thus nurturing a deeper, unshakeable faith.

Building this dependency into our lives means incorporating practical acts of faith. Prayer and meditation on God's Word are key practices. Through prayer, we communicate our needs and express our trust in God's providence. This dialogue aligns our hearts with The Lord's will and reminds us that He is in control. Regular meditation on Scriptures that highlight God's provision strengthens our faith and guides our thoughts.

Acknowledging our vulnerabilities and shortcomings reinforces our need for God's help. This humility is vital because it places us in a posture to receive God's grace. In accepting that we can't do it all alone, we open ourselves up to The Lord's divine intervention, fostering a deeper sense of trust and reliance. Testimonies and stories of God's provision play a critical role in cultivating a dependency mindset. Sharing these stories within our communities builds collective faith and reminds us of God's faithfulness. It's in hearing how God's hand has moved in others' lives that we find the encouragement to believe He will do the same for us. This communal faith-building enriches our individual journeys, grounding us further in the assurance of God's provision.

Another essential aspect is recognizing that provision from God sometimes comes in forms we don't expect. It's not always about material wealth; sometimes it's about spiritual insight, wisdom, or opportunities for personal growth. By staying attuned to the different ways God provides, we broaden our understanding of The Lord's care and recognize The Lord's hand even in the small, seemingly mundane aspects of our lives. This broader view helps us see that The Lord's provision is all-encompassing and always for our good.

Finally, we cultivate dependency on God through acts of gratitude. Regularly giving thanks for what we have transforms our perspective and aligns us more closely with God's heart. A grateful heart is fertile ground for faith because it acknowledges that everything we have already comes from God's hand. It involves reorienting our understanding of provision, engaging in practical acts of faith, sharing testimonies, recognizing God's diverse forms of provision, and practicing gratitude. By integrating these elements into our daily lives, we grow in faith and confidence, assured that God is our ultimate provider.

Daily Declaration for Trusting In Generosity

A Daily Declaration for Trusting in Generosity is a practice that reinforces the belief that when we give freely and with an open heart, we not only bless others but also trust in a greater system of reciprocity and divine provision. It is a statement of faith that acknowledges the powerful connection between generosity and abundance, both spiritually and materially. By making this declaration, we shift our mindset from one of scarcity and self-preservation to one of abundance and trust, believing that as we give, we will also receive.

At its core, trusting in generosity means believing that there is more than enough to go around and that our act of giving does not diminish our own resources but instead expands our capacity to receive. When we declare daily, "I trust that as I give, I will receive in return," we align ourselves with the principle that generosity breeds abundance. This affirmation serves as a reminder that the world operates on cycles of giving and receiving, and by participating in this flow, we position ourselves to experience more blessings.

Generosity, when rooted in trust, also reflects our faith in a higher power to meet our needs. By declaring, "I trust in God's provision as I give freely," we acknowledge that we are not the sole source of our wealth or well-being. Instead, we rely on the belief that God, or the universe, will continue to provide for us as we give to others. This shifts the focus away from hoarding or protecting our resources and allows us to give with a heart full of faith and confidence, knowing that our needs will be met in ways we may not always predict.

This declaration also has the power to transform how we view our role in the lives of others. By affirming, "I am a vessel of blessing to those around me," we recognize that generosity is not just about financial giving but also about offering time, support, kindness, and compassion. It encourages us to see ourselves as conduits through which blessings flow, allowing us to make a positive impact on the world while trusting that we, too, will be taken care of. This perspective cultivates a sense of purpose and fulfillment as we understand that our giving is part of a larger, divine plan.

Moreover, this daily declaration helps break the chains of fear and scarcity thinking. Often, people hesitate to give generously because they fear they won't have enough left for themselves. However, by declaring each day, "I trust that there is always enough," we begin to let go of those fears and embrace the truth that abundance is not finite. We remind ourselves that generosity leads to greater joy, peace, and abundance—not because of a transactional expectation but because we are living in alignment with spiritual laws that encourage giving freely and cheerfully.

This practice of daily declaration reinforces the idea that generosity is an act of faith, not merely an obligation. It shifts our giving from being driven by duty to being inspired by trust. By saying, "I give with a joyful heart, knowing that all is well," we embrace the joy and satisfaction that comes from giving out of love and faith, rather than from a sense of obligation or expectation of return.

Daily Declaration for Trusting in Generosity is a powerful affirmation that encourages a mindset of abundance, faith, and selflessness. It reminds us that giving is not only an act of kindness but also an expression of our trust in divine provision. By making this declaration each day, we open ourselves to receiving more blessings, foster a spirit of generosity, and live with greater peace and confidence that as we give, so too will we receive.

I Declare According to Philippians 4:19 Daily Provisions

In the ebbs and flows of our daily lives, we often find ourselves grappling with uncertainties and the relentless need for provision. Whether it's food on the table, a roof over our heads, or the emotional strength to face the day, our needs can feel overwhelming. Understanding the cultural perspective on provision requires us to shift our mindset from self-reliance to divine dependence. This is where Philippians 4:19 steps in, providing a pivotal reminder: "But my God shall supply all your need according to his riches in glory by Christ Jesus" (Philippians 4:19).

Understanding provision through a cultural or spiritual lens invites us to move beyond the confines of self-reliance toward a deeper, more profound trust in divine provision. Many cultures, particularly those rooted in faith, teach that provision is not simply the result of hard work or material success but is ultimately a gift from a higher power. This shift in mindset allows us to see ourselves not as the sole providers of our needs but as recipients of God's abundant resources. It reorients our perspective, acknowledging that while our efforts are important, it is God who sustains and supplies us with what we need.

This is where Philippians 4:19 becomes a crucial reminder: "But my God shall supply all your need according to his riches in glory by Christ Jesus." This verse underscores the truth that God, in His infinite wealth and glory, is more than capable of meeting all our needs. It takes the burden off our shoulders, replacing our fears about scarcity with the assurance that God's resources are boundless. Unlike human resources, which are finite and subject to depletion, God's provision is limitless, and His willingness to provide for us comes from His rich storehouses in heaven.

By leaning into this promise, we are invited to trust in something greater than ourselves. Rather than being consumed by the pressures of everyday life, we can find peace in the knowledge that God will provide exactly what we need, when we need it. This doesn't mean we become passive or stop putting in effort, but it frees us from the anxiety that comes from trying to control every aspect of our provision. It teaches us to focus on our relationship with God, knowing that He cares for us deeply and will provide according to His perfect timing and wisdom.

Let's unpack this for a moment. The notion that God will provide all our needs according to The Lord's riches invites us into an abundant mindset. It clashes against the scarcity culture we often encounter, which tells us there's never enough to go around. By declaring daily that our needs are met by God's abundant riches, we begin to cultivate a mindset of trust and generosity. This declaration isn't just a statement; it's a transformative belief that aligns us with divine provision.

Imagine walking into each day with the unshakeable assurance that your needs are already met. This doesn't mean we sit back and do nothing, but rather, it means our efforts are partnered with a greater source. When we declare Philippians 4:19 over our lives, we're actively choosing to step out of anxiety and step into faith. This daily declaration forms the root of our trust in divine abundance, paving the way for both practical and spiritual provision.

It's essential to understand that the cultural perspective on provision varies widely. Some cultures emphasize self-reliance and the "pull yourself up by your bootstraps" mentality, while others lean heavily on communal support and shared wealth. While these perspectives offer valuable insights, embracing the concept of divine provision through Philippians 4:19 transcends cultural limitations. It reminds us that regardless of our background or current situation, there is a higher source committed to our well-being.

Intertwining this declaration with our daily routines also changes how we view generosity. When we're secure in the knowledge that our needs are met, we are more inclined to share our resources with others. This aligns with the biblical principle found in Luke 6:38: "Give, and it shall be given unto you; good measure, pressed down, and shaken together, and running over..." (Luke 6:38). The act of giving, inspired by our trust in God's provision, becomes an overflow of the abundance we trust God to provide.

However, trusting in generosity and God's provision doesn't exempt us from challenges. There will be days when the bank account runs low or the emotional reservoir feels depleted. Yet, this is where our daily declaration finds its power. By consistently affirming that God will supply all our needs, we fortify our spirit against the ebb and flow of life's circumstances.

Think about it: how would your life change if you truly believed that all your needs were already accounted for? This belief could transform not only your approach to personal challenges but also how you engage with your community. When a culture of generosity is cultivated, both individuals and societies benefit. This aligns with the broader goal of this book—to help readers achieve a life of Spiritual, Financial, and Mental Wellness. Our declarations are not just about personal gain; they are about fostering a culture that benefits everyone.

The power of daily declarations lies in their ability to reshape our thinking and, consequently, our actions. Philippians 4:19 serves as a cornerstone for this, affirming that God's provision isn't limited or scarce. It's a daily reminder that we are connected to an inexhaustible source. As you incorporate this declaration into your life, let it guide you in moments of doubt and help you cultivate a mindset of openness and trust.

We often limit our perspective of provision to material needs, but God's care extends beyond that. Emotional, spiritual, and relational needs are also encompassed in The Lord's promise. By declaring, "My God shall supply all your need according to his riches in glory by Christ Jesus," we affirm that every facet of our lives is under divine care. This comprehensive provision enables us to navigate life with a sense of peace and purpose. This declaration roots us in the belief that God's provision is not a temporary fix but a sustainable source of support. This is a crucial aspect of cultivating a mindset of dependency on God. When we recognize that The Lord's generosity is unending, we can lean into a life marked by less stress and more gratitude. The narrative shifts from one of constant striving to one of blessed assurance.

In terms of practical application, consider setting aside time each day to meditate on Philippians 4:19 and speak it aloud. Let it infuse your morning routine, frame your day, and be the last thought as you drift off to sleep. The consistency of this practice can shift your heart and mind to align more closely with divine truth. In doing so, you create a spiritual rhythm that underpins your daily actions and decisions.

Anxiety about provision is a common human experience, exacerbated by societal pressures and personal expectations. Yet, by embracing this daily declaration, you invite a renewed sense of calm into your life. Philippians 4:19 serves as a divine antidote to worry, replacing it with confidence in God's faithful provision. This doesn't mean challenges disappear, but it does mean you face them with newfound courage and trust.

Finally, it's important to remember that declarations are not merely about repeating words; they are about embodying them. Live out the truth of Philippians 4:19 in your actions. Practice generosity, knowing you are backed by divine abundance. Cultivate gratitude daily, recognizing the myriad ways God fulfills The Lord's promises. By doing so, you not only transform your life but also become a beacon of hope and trust for others.

In these ways, the Daily Declaration for Trusting In Generosity becomes more than a statement—it becomes a lifestyle. Through the lens of Philippians 4:19, we are invited to live from a place of assured provision, unshakable trust, and impactful generosity. This transformative journey aligns perfectly with our goal of achieving a successful life in wisdom, wealth and wellness. Embrace this declaration wholeheartedly, and watch as it changes your perspective, your actions, and ultimately, your life.

Wellness Points:

1. Daily Declaration: Declare according to Philippians 4:19 daily provisions.

2. Cultural Heritage: Embrace and honor your cultural heritage while integrating biblical principles into your life.

3. Faith in Provision: Cultivate a mindset of trust and faith in God's provision for all your needs.

4. Generational Wisdom: Pass down the wisdom and traditions of your cultural heritage alongside biblical teachings.

5. Holistic Well-being: Strive for a holistic approach to well-being that includes spiritual, cultural, and financial aspects.

Wellness Questions:

1. How does your cultural background influence your understanding of provision and wealth?

____

____

____

2. What practices can you adopt to cultivate a mindset of dependency on God for daily provision?

____

____

____

3. How do you balance cultural traditions with biblical principles in your approach to wealth and provision?

____

____

____

4. In what ways can you use your cultural heritage to enrich your spiritual and financial well-being?

____

____

____

5. How can you create a legacy that honors both your cultural heritage and your faith?

____

____

____

Wellness Notes:

CHAPTER 8:
INTEGRATING A LIFE OF SUCCESS

Embarking upon a journey that simultaneously binds wisdom, wealth, and wellness requires a life-altering transformation. These crucial elements, when harmonized, produce a resonance that awakens the most profound potential within us. In this chapter, we blend these elements to create a holistic approach to success.

By harmonizing these elements, we unlock the profound potential within us. We learn to live with purpose, guided by wisdom, supported by financial abundance, and sustained by a deep sense of well-being. This transformative approach not only enhances our personal lives but also enables us to positively impact those around us, creating a ripple effect of growth, health, and prosperity in our families, communities, and beyond. It is through this union of wisdom, wealth, and wellness that we find true fulfillment and the ability to navigate life's complexities with grace and power.

First, let's consider wisdom. Proverbs tells us, "Happy is the man that findeth wisdom, and the man that getteth understanding" (Prov. 3:13). Obtaining wisdom isn't merely about accumulating knowledge; it's about applying that knowledge to lead a life aligned with divine purpose. It's the guiding star, enabling us to discern right from wrong and to navigate life's challenges with grace. In incorporating wisdom, you must remember that it's an everyday act—a conscious choice to seek understanding and apply it consistently.

As we integrate wealth into this tripod, it's essential to break free from misconceptions about prosperity. Money isn't the root of all evil; rather, the love of money is (1 Tim. 6:10). True wealth encompasses far more than material riches. It's about creating a life where financial stability enables freedom, generosity, and growth. When we talk about wealth, think of it as a resource that supports your mission, allowing you to focus on higher goals without being burdened by financial constraints. Building wealth is akin to building a legacy that enables you and those who come after you to thrive.

Your physical wellness is the vessel through which all other achievements are channeled, and your mental wellbeing is the lens through which you view your world. Health isn't a separate entity; it's an integral part of wisdom and wealth. Without wellness, both wisdom and wealth lose their value, for they cannot be fully enjoyed or utilized.

So, how do we interweave these threads seamlessly? It starts with a holistic approach to daily living. You cannot focus on one element while neglecting the others. Picture this as a daily practice rather than an end goal. Each decision you make, be it about your finances, your health, or the wisdom you seek, should consider the effects on the other two elements. By doing so, you create a balanced life that reflects your core values and divine purpose.

Let's illustrate this with a practical scenario. Imagine making a career choice. The wisdom aspect would prompt you to seek understanding and guidance in making the right decision. The wealth component would involve evaluating the financial implications and how it aligns with your long-term goals. Lastly, wellness would ensure that your choice supports your mental and physical health, preventing burnout and promoting sustained growth.

This brings us to our daily declaration: "I Declare According to 3rd John 1:2 A Life of Success, Defined By My Purpose, Measured in My Obedience and Fulfilled With My Potential." This declaration is more than words; it's a covenant with your holistic being. It calls you to live a life where your wisdom drives your decisions, your wealth empowers your actions, and your wellness sustains your journey.

Integrating these aspects goes beyond personal fulfillment; it impacts those around you. By embodying wisdom, wealth, and wellness, you exemplify a life well-lived, inspiring others to strive for their own holistic success. You become a beacon of what is possible, a living testament to 3 John 1:2's promise and a steward of your blessings.

As you move forward, remember this balance. When one aspect flourishes, ensure it nourishes the others. This triune integration is a divine design, promoting a life that is not just lived, but lived abundantly. "For where your treasure is, there will your heart be also" (Matt. 6:21). Place your treasure in Spiritual, Financial, and Mental Wellness, and watch your life transform into a harmonious symphony of purpose, abundance, and vitality.

Allow this chapter to be a guidepost as you navigate the dynamic currents of life. Embrace the interconnected nature of Spiritual, Financial, and Mental Wellness. By doing so, you honor not only your own life but the divine blueprint laid out for you. Live a life balanced with wisdom, enriched with wealth, and sustained by wellness, for this is the path to true, enduring success.

Daily Declaration for Practical Implementation

A Daily Declaration for Practical Implementation is a powerful tool for bridging the gap between intention and action. It serves as a focused affirmation that aligns your goals, mindset, and daily habits with a commitment to taking tangible steps toward achieving success. While declarations often focus on positive thinking and belief in oneself, a declaration for practical implementation goes beyond mere affirmations. It emphasizes the importance of translating intentions into specific, actionable steps that lead to real progress in various aspects of life, whether they are personal, professional, or spiritual.

At the heart of this declaration is the recognition that success requires not only vision and planning but also consistent execution. By starting your day with a declaration like, "Today, I commit to taking practical steps toward my goals," you mentally prepare yourself to move beyond wishful thinking and focus on the actions necessary to bring your aspirations to life. This type of declaration transforms abstract desires into concrete outcomes, encouraging a proactive mindset that seeks solutions, embraces discipline, and maintains momentum.

Practical implementation means focusing on daily habits that accumulate over time and lead to long-term success. By making this declaration a part of your routine, you commit to small, achievable tasks that, when compounded, create significant progress. This might involve setting aside time for focused work on a project, scheduling a workout for physical health, or dedicating moments to spiritual practices such as prayer or meditation. Each step you take, however small, brings you closer to your larger goals, and the daily declaration serves as a reminder to stay consistent and disciplined.

The declaration also promotes accountability. When you affirm each day that you will take practical steps toward your goals, you hold yourself accountable for following through. This is particularly useful in preventing procrastination, as it shifts your focus from distant outcomes to the immediate actions that need to be taken today. By committing to this declaration, you are constantly reminded that success is not achieved by waiting for the right circumstances but by actively creating the conditions for it through intentional effort.

Another key element of this daily declaration is adaptability. Practical implementation often requires flexibility, as not all plans unfold as expected. By declaring each morning that you will take practical steps, you prepare yourself to adapt when necessary, ensuring that setbacks or obstacles do not derail your progress. The declaration helps cultivate a mindset that is both goal-oriented and open to adjusting strategies when needed, allowing for resilience in the face of challenges. This daily practice reinforces the principle of focus. In a world full of distractions, a declaration for practical implementation helps sharpen your attention on what truly matters. It reminds you to prioritize tasks that align with your core goals and to eliminate activities that do not contribute to your progress. By making this a daily affirmation, you cultivate the habit of intentional living, where every action is purpose-driven and aligned with your greater vision.

By affirming that you will take practical steps today, you balance the tension between effort and faith, understanding that while you are responsible for the actions, the ultimate results may unfold in unexpected ways. This trust allows you to release the anxiety of perfectionism and embrace the process of growth, knowing that consistent implementation will yield progress over time.

Holistic Approach to Success

As we delve into the harmonious integration of wisdom, wealth, and wellness, it becomes crucial to focus on practical implementation. The declaration "I declare according to 3rd John 1:2 a life of success, defined by my purpose, measured in my obedience, and fulfilled with my potential," serves as a profound testament to what we aspire to achieve. In this journey, 3rd John 1:2 states, "Beloved, I wish above all things that thou mayest prosper and be in health, even as thy soul prospereth" (3 John 1:2).

Success is not merely about accolades or material gains; it's intricately woven into our purpose. Identifying your unique purpose is the first step towards genuine success. Reflect on the talents, passions, and callings that God has bestowed upon you. Scripture attests, "For we are his workmanship, created in Christ Jesus unto good works, which God hath before ordained that we should walk in them" (Eph. 2:10). Embrace this divine craftsmanship in your journey of purpose.

The journey toward this deeper form of success begins with reflection on the gifts, passions, and callings that God has given each of us. These are not random or insignificant aspects of who we are; they are part of our divine design. As Ephesians 2:10 declares, "For we are his workmanship, created in Christ Jesus unto good works, which God hath before ordained that we should walk in them." This scripture reminds us that we are God's handiwork, intricately crafted with intention and purpose. Our talents, passions, and even our struggles are all part of this divine workmanship, pointing us toward the good works that God has prepared for us to accomplish.

I Declare According to 3rd John 1:2 A Life of Success, Defined By My Purpose, Measured in My Obedience and Fulfilled With My Potential

Understanding that we are God's workmanship means recognizing the significance of the gifts we have been given. These gifts—whether artistic, intellectual, relational, or spiritual—are the tools through which we can fulfill our purpose. They are not merely for our own personal enjoyment or success but are meant to serve a greater good, to bring light and positivity into the world, and to align with God's plan for us. Identifying these gifts requires a deep level of self-reflection and prayer, as we seek to understand what we are passionate about and how we can use those passions to serve others and glorify God.

Furthermore, aligning with our purpose gives us clarity and direction in life. When we are unsure of our purpose, we often chase superficial measures of success—money, recognition, or approval from others. But when we understand that success is about walking in the path that God has ordained for us, we find peace and satisfaction, regardless of whether we receive external accolades. Our purpose becomes our compass, guiding us through life's decisions, challenges, and opportunities. This understanding allows us to embrace success not as something measured by worldly standards but as living fully into the life that God has designed for us.

Embracing our divine craftsmanship also means accepting that our purpose may not always align with society's definitions of success. It requires courage to pursue a path that is uniquely ours, even when it doesn't conform to the expectations of others. But as we trust in God's design, we realize that walking in our purpose brings a level of fulfillment that no amount of material gain or public recognition can offer. It is in this alignment with God's will that we find true success— success that is rich in meaning, impact, and spiritual depth.

Success that is woven into our purpose is the kind of success that leads to genuine fulfillment and joy. It requires us to reflect on the talents, passions, and callings that God has entrusted to us and to embrace these gifts as part of His divine craftsmanship. As Ephesians 2:10 affirms, we are created for good works that God has prepared for us to walk in, and it is in walking this path of purpose that we experience true success. When we live in alignment with our purpose, we not only find personal satisfaction but also contribute to the greater good, leaving a lasting impact that reflects the divine design of our lives.

Once you've identified your purpose, practice obedience. The Bible reminds us, "If ye be willing and obedient, ye shall eat the good of the land" (Isa. 1:19). Obedience isn't just about following rules but about aligning your actions with the higher calling you've discovered. It's through this alignment that you unlock untapped potential and move toward a life marked by profound fulfillment. Every step of obedience is a step closer to manifesting the wisdom, wealth, and wellness designed for you.

Obedience to your purpose is the process of actively choosing to honor the gifts, passions, and callings that God has placed within you. It's about making decisions that reflect your commitment to this purpose, even when the path may be difficult or uncertain. This is where obedience requires faith, as it involves trusting that every step you take in alignment with your purpose is guiding you closer to the life you are meant to lead. It is through these steps of obedience that your purpose begins to manifest in tangible ways, shaping the direction of your life.

As you practice obedience, you also unlock untapped potential within yourself. Often, we are unaware of the depth of our capabilities until we are fully aligned with our purpose and take bold steps of obedience toward it. This process reveals strengths, talents, and wisdom that may have been dormant because they were not yet needed. But as you walk in obedience, you activate these aspects of your potential, allowing them to flourish and contribute to your growth. Each act of obedience is a demonstration of faith, and as you take these steps, God provides the resources, wisdom, and opportunities you need to continue progressing on your path.

Obedience aligns you with divine timing and provision. When your actions are in harmony with your purpose, you are no longer striving in your own strength or chasing success as defined by external standards. Instead, you are working in sync with a higher plan. This brings a sense of peace and flow to your life, as you trust that your needs—whether spiritual, financial, or emotional—will be met. Obedience positions you to receive the wisdom, wealth, and wellness that God has designed for you, as it signals your readiness to handle these blessings responsibly.

Every step of obedience is a step closer to manifesting the fullness of your purpose. It is not always a grand or dramatic gesture; often, obedience involves small, everyday decisions that reflect your commitment to living with integrity and purpose. Over time, these small acts accumulate, shaping the course of your life and leading to significant breakthroughs. Obedience also requires perseverance, especially when the journey becomes challenging or unclear. However, each step strengthens your faith, builds character, and moves you toward the life of wisdom, wealth, and wellness that is part of your divine design.

Aligning your life with your purpose also means embracing the process, despite its challenges. Not every day will be victorious, and some days may feel like setbacks. But scriptural wisdom such as "But they that wait upon the Lord shall renew their strength; they shall mount up with wings as eagles; they shall run, and not be weary; and they shall walk, and not faint" (Isa. 40:31), gives us the strength to carry on. Consistent adherence to your purpose fortifies your journey, ensuring that setbacks become stepping stones.

When success is viewed through the lens of divine purpose, it transcends temporal achievements. It becomes about the quality of our obedience and the fulfillment of our God-given potential. Each morning, declare this affirmation and realign your day to step into the success measured by God's standards. Remember, success is fluid and redefined as you grow deeper in understanding your purpose.

The integration of wisdom, wealth, and wellness starts in the mind and spirit. Scripture accentuates the importance of mindset in achieving true prosperity. "For as he thinketh in his heart, so is he" (Prov. 23:7). It means cultivating a mindset that reflects God's promises and walking in those promises daily. Each thought should be in alignment with the divine roadmap provided to us through scripture.

Potential is fulfilled not by chance but by deliberate action infused with wisdom. "The heart of the prudent getteth knowledge; and the ear of the wise seeketh knowledge" (Prov. 18:15). Seek knowledge in every area of life, be it spiritual, financial, or physical. Make learning a daily habit, reinforcing your declarations with actions grounded in wisdom and truth.

To unlock potential, it is essential to become a lifelong learner, constantly seeking knowledge in all areas of life—spiritual, financial, physical, and emotional. Success, in any form, begins with understanding that the more you know, the more equipped you are to navigate challenges, make sound decisions, and grow in all aspects of life. Spiritual potential is deepened through studying sacred texts, engaging in prayer or meditation, and learning from spiritual mentors who guide you in faith and purpose. Financial potential grows as you seek wisdom in managing resources, learning about investments, and making responsible, informed decisions. Similarly, physical well-being and potential are maximized by gaining knowledge on health, nutrition, and fitness, and applying those insights in your daily routine.

Learning should become a daily habit, not something reserved for formal education or specific life stages. When you make learning a priority, you continually sharpen your skills, deepen your understanding, and broaden your perspective. This deliberate pursuit of knowledge empowers you to align your actions with wisdom, ensuring that every decision you make is thoughtful, informed, and in service of your larger purpose. Whether it's reading books, attending seminars, seeking mentors, or simply being open to new ideas, learning consistently reinforces your growth. It allows you to adapt, innovate, and approach life's challenges with confidence and insight.

Each day, let your declarations become the catalyst for action. Write them down, speak them aloud, and live them out. Form a habit, and let these declarations renew your mind daily. Align your thoughts, words, and actions with the declaration from 3rd John 1:2, fostering a holistic environment for integrating wisdom, wealth, and wellness.

In essence, potential is fulfilled not by taking deliberate action. Seeking knowledge ensures that you are always growing, adapting, and moving closer to your goals. As you make learning a daily habit and reinforce your declarations with wise, purposeful actions, you set the foundation for fulfilling your potential in all aspects of life. Through this intentional pursuit of knowledge and wisdom, you align yourself with the truth and power needed to bring your potential to life.

This journey isn't just an end but a new beginning. Commit daily to this declaration and let it shape the landscape of your life, ensuring success as defined by your purpose and obedience. Remember, it's a divine journey, and every step you take brings you closer to fulfilling your God-given potential.

Each day, let your declarations become the catalyst for action. Write them down, speak them aloud, and live them out. Form a habit, and let these declarations renew your mind daily. Align your thoughts, words, and actions with the declaration from 3rd John 1:2, fostering a holistic environment for integrating wisdom, wealth, and wellness.

In a world full of fleeting fads and temporal successes, ground yourself in declarations backed by scripture. "Heaven and earth shall pass away: but my words shall not pass away" (Matt. 24:35). God's promises are eternal; therefore, declarations rooted in scripture hold everlasting power. Reflect on these words daily, letting them affirm your purpose and guide your actions.

Concluding this journey isn't just an end but a new beginning. Commit daily to these declaration and let it shape the landscape of your life, ensuring success as defined by your purpose and obedience. Remember, it's a divine journey, and every step you take brings you closer to fulfilling your God-given potential.

Wellness Points:

1. Daily Declaration: Declare according to 3 John 1:2 a life of success defined by purpose, obedience, and potential.

2. Holistic Approach: Adopt a holistic approach to success that includes spiritual, emotional, and financial health.

3. Balance and Prioritization: Prioritize balance in your life, ensuring that no single aspect of well-being is neglected.

4. Community Contribution: Use your resources and talents to contribute to the well-being of your community.

5. Continuous Growth: Commit to continuous growth in wisdom, aligning your life with divine principles and purpose.

Wellness Questions:

1. How can you create a balanced approach to life that integrates wisdom, wealth, and wellness?

    ____

    ____

    ____

2. What practices can you adopt to ensure your pursuit of wealth does not compromise your spiritual and emotional well-being?

    ____

    ____

    ____

3. How do you measure success in a way that includes spiritual, emotional, and financial health?

    ____

    ____

    ____

4. In what ways can you use your resources to promote holistic wellness in your community?

    ____

    ____

    ____

5. How can you continuously grow in wisdom while maintaining financial stability and emotional health?

    ____

    ____

    ____

Wellness Notes:

CONCLUSION

The journey through the chapters of this book has been an enlightening odyssey, designed to guide you towards a life rich in wisdom, wealth, and wellness. We've delved into the essence of self-worth, the importance of wisdom, the nurturing of emotional and mental health, and the path to spiritual wellness. We've discussed the significance of building wealth, not just for yourself but for future generations, and the cultural importance of relying on divine provision. This final chapter brings all these elements together, emphasizing that a holistic approach is paramount.

In our pursuit of a successful life, let's remember the words of Jeremiah 29:11: "For I know the thoughts that I think toward you, saith the Lord, thoughts of peace, and not of evil, to give you an expected end" (Jer. 29:11). The wisdom encapsulated in these words reassures us that our efforts, when aligned with divine purpose, lead toward fulfillment and peace. This life is a complex tapestry, and each thread—whether it be wisdom, wealth, or wellness—must be woven with intention and care. Each daily declaration you've learned is a step in reinforcing these threads, binding them together in a robust and unbreakable pattern.

The progress you make in your personal and professional life is a testament to your dedication and belief. Each affirmation spoken guides your thoughts and actions towards positive outcomes. Ecclesiastes 9:10 reminds us: "Whatsoever thy hand findeth to do, do it with thy might" (Eccl. 9:10), underlining the importance of diligent effort. Your path to greatness is paved with the declarations you've adopted, standing as beacons of faith and determination.

Building a successful life involves more than individual effort; it demands a community and sometimes, a mentor. Reflecting on Proverbs 27:17, "Iron sharpeneth iron; so a man sharpeneth the countenance of his friend" (Prov. 27:17), it's clear that success is often born from mutual support and shared wisdom. Cultivate relationships that encourage growth and help you maintain your course. These alliances will strengthen your resolve as you face life's challenges.

Unlocking the full potential of your life also means understanding the spiritual dimensions of existence. Jesus said in John 10:10: "I am come that they might have life, and that they might have it more abundantly" (John 10:10). Embrace the spiritual tools available to you and seek a deeper connection with your faith. This inner growth is not just supplementary but foundational to achieving all other forms of success.

Your financial wellbeing, as discussed, is crucial. Wealth goes beyond mere accumulation; it's about the legacy you leave behind. It's about ensuring that your children and their children experience the benefits of your hard work. Proverbs 13:22 tells us, "A good man leaveth an inheritance to his children's children" (Prov. 13:22). Focus on financial wisdom to create generational wealth that uplifts and inspires long after you're gone.

Emotional and mental wellness is equally critical. In Proverbs 17:22, we read, "A merry heart doeth good like a medicine: but a broken spirit drieth the bones" (Prov. 17:22). This highlights the importance of nurturing a joyful and positive mindset. A balanced state of mind enhances your capacity for resilience and creativity, equipping you to handle life's vicissitudes with grace and fortitude.

To keep the flame of success burning bright, remember the holistic approach echoed throughout this book. Integrating wisdom, wealth, and wellness isn't just a strategy; it's a lifestyle. Each aspect supports the other, creating a harmonious balance that leads to sustained success. James 1:5 advises, "If any of you lack wisdom, let him ask of God, that giveth to all men liberally, and upbraideth not; and it shall be given him" (James 1:5). Seek divine guidance in unifying these principles within your life.

As you conclude this journey and move forward, it's imperative to maintain a focus on purpose and potential. Colossians 3:23 states, "And whatsoever ye do, do it heartily, as to the Lord, and not unto men" (Col. 3:23). This emphasizes dedicating all efforts to a higher purpose, which ultimately leads to a more rewarding and meaningful life.

With every step, every declaration, and every realized goal, you grow closer to the vision of success defined by the values discussed. The time spent has not been in vain; rather, it has been an investment in building a future that mirrors divine promises and your highest aspirations. Remember Philippians 4:13, "I can do all things through Christ which strengtheneth me" (Phil. 4:13). Let this be your mantra as you continue to build a life that is truly successful.

As we part ways in this literary journey, continue to speak these affirmations over your life. They are not mere words but powerful tools given to you for transformation. We conclude with the faith that you've not just read these pages, but that you've internalized their message, prepared to walk in the fullness of spiritual fulfillment.

Continued Practice of Affirmations: As you conclude this literary journey, the practice of speaking affirmations should continue to be a vital part of your daily routine. These affirmations are more than just spoken words; they are declarations of faith and truth that have the power to shape your reality. By consistently speaking these affirmations, you reinforce the positive messages and principles discussed throughout the book, ensuring that they take root and grow in your life.

The affirmations provided are designed to be transformative. They serve as powerful tools to realign your thoughts, attitudes, and actions with godly principles. Each affirmation is a seed of change, capable of producing significant growth and transformation in your spiritual, financial, and mental well-being. When spoken with conviction and faith, these affirmations can break down negative thought patterns, build up your self-esteem, and guide you towards making wise and fruitful decisions.

The goal of this book is not only for you to read and understand its content but to internalize its message. As you internalize these affirmations and the principles behind them, you prepare yourself to walk in the fullness of wellness. Spiritual wellness comes from a deeper connection with God and a strong sense of purpose. Financial wellness is achieved through wise stewardship and trust in God's provision. Mental wellness is fostered by maintaining a positive and resilient mindset. By embracing and living out these affirmations, you position yourself to experience a holistic sense of wellness, walking confidently in the fullness of life that God intends for you.

Let's hold fast to the words of 3 John 1:2: "Beloved, I wish above all things that thou mayest prosper and be in health, even as thy soul prospereth" (3 John 1:2). Let this declaration be the cornerstone of your pursuit, aligning your worldly success with spiritual fulfillment.

May your journey be blessed and abundant. Amen.

Appendix A:
Appendix

Declarations for Wisdom, Wealth, & Wellness

I declare according to Psalm 139:14
that I am fearfully and wonderfully made

I declare according to Proverbs 4:23
control over my thoughts, words and ways

I declare according to Galatians 5:22-23
discernment in my choices

I declare according to Ephesians 1:3
access to spiritual blessings

I declare according to James 1:17
greatness and prosperity

I declare according to Deuteronomy 28: 3-4
generational blessings

I declare according to Philippians 4:19
daily provisions

According to 3rd John 1:2
I declare a life of success, defined by my purpose, measured in my obedience and fulfilled with my potential. This is my declaration, for wisdom, wealth, and wellness

Appendix B:
Appendix

In this Appendix, you'll find additional declarations designed to cater to various specific situations you might encounter on your journey to a successful life.

Declarations for Personal Growth

- **I declare according to Psalm 32:8**, that I will receive guidance and instruction from the Lord in every step I take. "I will instruct thee and teach thee in the way which thou shalt go: I will guide thee with mine eye" (Ps. 32:8).

- **I declare according to Philippians 4:13**, that I can do all things through Christ who gives me strength: "I can do all things through Christ which strengtheneth me" (Phil. 4:13).

Declarations for Overcoming Challenges

- **I declare according to Isaiah 41:10**, that I will not fear, for God is with me. "Fear thou not; for I am with thee: be not dismayed; for I am thy God: I will strengthen thee; yea, I will help thee; yea, I will uphold thee with the right hand of my righteousness" (Isa. 41:10).

- **I declare according to Romans 8:37**, that in all things I am more than a conqueror through Him who loved us. "Nay, in all these things we are more than conquerors through him that loved us" (Rom. 8:37).

Declarations for Relationships

- **I declare according to Ephesians 4:32**, that I will be kind, tenderhearted, and forgiving to others. "And be ye kind one to another, tenderhearted, forgiving one another, even as God for Christ's sake hath forgiven you" (Eph. 4:32).

- **I declare according to Colossians 3:14**, that I will put on love, which binds everything together in perfect harmony. "And above all these things put on charity, which is the bond of perfectness" (Col. 3:14).

Declarations for Health and Healing

- **I declare according to Jeremiah 30:17**, that the Lord will restore health unto me and heal my wounds. "For I will restore health unto thee, and I will heal thee of thy wounds, saith the Lord" (Jer. 30:17).

- **I declare according to 3 John 1:2**, that I will prosper and be in good health, even as my soul prospers. "Beloved, I wish above all things that thou mayest prosper and be in health, even as thy soul prospereth" (3 John 1:2).

Declarations for Financial Breakthrough

- **I declare according to Deuteronomy 8:18**, that the Lord gives me power to get wealth. "But thou shalt remember the Lord thy God: for it is he that giveth thee power to get wealth" (Deut. 8:18).

- **I declare according to Philippians 4:19**, that God will meet all my needs according to His riches in glory by Christ Jesus. "But my God shall supply all your need according to his riches in glory by Christ Jesus" (Phil. 4:19).

Additional Declarations for Specific Situations

In our journey through life, we often encounter moments that require us to draw upon reserves of strength, faith, and wisdom. It's during these times that tailored declarations can serve as powerful tools for guidance and encouragement. For specific situations, personalized declarations, based on scriptural truths, can act as beacons of hope and reminders of God's promises. They are not just words spoken into the air; they are affirmations rooted in the unshakeable truths of the Bible.

One of the most poignant circumstances where declarations wield immense power is in times of illness. Facing health challenges, either personally or within our family, can be daunting. Declaring healing and health over oneself or a loved one can help realign our faith. For instance, "I declare according to Isaiah 53:5, 'by His stripes, we are healed.'" This powerful promise can anchor us in hope and remind us of God's healing covenant.

Financial difficulties can weigh heavily on our minds and spirits. During such times, declarations about God's provision can be a source of comfort and direction. Proverbs 10:22 says, "The blessing of the Lord, it maketh rich, and he addeth no sorrow with it." By declaring these words, we remind ourselves that our future is secure in God's hands, shifting our minds from worry to faith.

Marital challenges are another area where declarations can profoundly impact. The institution of marriage, being under constant attack, needs the armor of affirmations. Declaring unity and understanding, as reflected in Ephesians 4:2-3, "With all lowliness and meekness, with longsuffering, forbearing one another in love; Endeavoring to keep the unity of the Spirit in the bond of peace," can strengthen the marital bond and remind couples of their commitment to each other.

Parenting, with its joys and trials, often requires divine wisdom and patience. Declarations for wisdom in parenting can bring reassurance. Proverbs 22:6 advises, "Train up a child in the way he should go: and when he is old, he will not depart from it." By speaking forth this truth, parents affirm their trust in God's guidance, ensuring they make godly decisions in nurturing their children.

Career and vocational aspirations also benefit from declarations. As we seek to fulfill our professional callings, it's essential to invite God's favor and direction. Declaring, "I can do all things through Christ which strengtheneth me" (Phil. 4:13), serves not just as motivation but as a reminder of the divine empowerment available in our endeavors.

Faced with grief and loss, it's natural to feel overwhelmed by sorrow. However, declarations based on God's comfort can offer solace. "Blessed are they that mourn: for they shall be comforted" (Matt. 5:4) reminds us of God's ever-present compassion, providing strength and hope in the midst of heartache.

Forgiveness is another critical component often needed in various contexts. Carrying unforgiveness can weigh down the soul, but declarations can help release those burdens. By saying, "And be ye kind one to another, tenderhearted, forgiving one another, even as God for Christ's sake hath forgiven you" (Eph. 4:32), we remind ourselves of the grace we've received and the importance of extending it to others.

In times of fear and anxiety, declarations anchored in God's protection and peace can provide much-needed reassurance. "Yea, though I walk through the valley of the shadow of death, I will fear no evil: for thou art with me; thy rod and thy staff they comfort me" (Psalm 23:4) serves as a potent reminder of God's presence, diminishing the power of fear over our minds and hearts.

The pursuit of personal dreams and ambitions is another arena where declarations can play a pivotal role. By affirming, "For I know the plans I have for you, declares the Lord, plans to prosper you and not to harm you, plans to give you hope and a future" (Jer. 29:11), one can reinforce their faith in God's perfect timing and plans, fostering perseverance and hope.

For those embarking on new beginnings, whether it's moving to a new place, starting a new job, or entering a new season of life, declarations can provide grounding and optimism. A declaration such as "Behold, I will do a new thing; now it shall spring forth; shall ye not know it? I will even make a way in the wilderness, and rivers in the desert" (Isaiah 43:19) affirms God's role in paving new paths and bringing forth opportunities.

Relationships, whether within families, friendships, or communities, thrive on harmony and understanding. Declarations promoting peace and unity, like "Blessed are the peacemakers: for they shall be called the children of God" (Matt. 5:9), encourage behaviors and attitudes that foster reconciliation and cooperation among individuals.

These additional declarations are more than words; they are lifelines and beacons, illuminating the path toward wisdom, wealth, and wellness. Through the power of spoken words, rooted in Scripture, we align our hearts and minds with God's truths, claiming His promises for every situation we face.